They're All in It Together

❏

They're All in It Together
When Good Things Happen to Bad People

Donald W. Kaul
Edited by Christopher Kaul

Andrews and McMeel

A Universal Press Syndicate Company
Kansas City

Library of Congress Cataloging-in-Publication Data

Kaul, Donald.
    They're all in it together : when good things happen to bad people
/ Donald W. Kaul : edited by Christopher Kaul.
        p.   cm.
    ISBN 0-8362-6220-4 : $16.95
    1. United States—Politics and government—1981–1989.   2. Politicians—
United States.   3. World politics—1975–1985.   4. World politics—
1985–1995.   I. Kaul, Christopher.   II. Title.
E876.K387   1991
320.973—dc20   91-28179
                                                                     CIP

Attention: Schools and Businesses

Andrews and McMeel books are available at quantity discounts with
bulk purchase for educational, business, or sales promotional use.
For information, please write to: Special Sales Department,
Andrews and McMeel, 4900 Main Street, Kansas City, Missouri 64112.

To my wife, Sue, who has
suffered through this book and
much more with humor and grace.

CONTENTS

INTRODUCTION
ix

1.
A MAN FOR ONE SEASON
1

2.
THE BUSH THING
23

3.
THERE IS A BOMB IN GILEAD
44

4.
DAS KAPITAL, GERFLUNKEN
55

5.
FATHERS AND SONS—AND DAUGHTERS
72

6.

GOD ISN'T DEAD, SHE'S ONLY SLEEPING
86

7.

WINNING ISN'T THE ONLY THING;
THERE'S LOSING, FOR EXAMPLE
111

8.

FOOLS, CHARLATANS, SCOUNDRELS
AND THE OTHER RECOGNIZED PROFESSIONS
124

9.

THE EVIL THAT MEN DO
141

10.

CANCEL MY APPOINTMENT IN SAMARA
153

INTRODUCTION

CALL ME ISHMAEL. No, wait a minute! Don't call me Ishmael. Let me try again.

You don't know about me lessen you read a book called . . .

No, that's no good either. Introductions are so difficult.

How do you do. My name is Donald Kaul, just as it says on the front of this book. I am a columnist, and this is a book of my columns.

It is a chain book. You are required to buy ten copies and send them to friends with the instructions that they each buy ten copies and send them to ten more friends, and so on. If you buy the books, good fortune will follow, and it will never rain on weekends. If you don't . . .

A society dentist in St. Joseph, Missouri, picked up a copy at his neighborhood bookstore and laid it back down. Within six months all of his patients' gums had receded—and his bank account with them.

On the other hand, an arc welder in Iron Mountain, Michigan, bought ten copies and soon after received a phone call from Ed Mac-Mahon. It's your decision; don't blow it.

But enough of you; what about me?

I grew up on the near-northwest side of Detroit in a Polish neighborhood. It was a childhood innocent of sophistication. My colleagues—Sonny, Stashu, Bernie and the rest—did not so much tell Polish jokes as live them.

Yet we were not stupid; we knew certain things, and one of them was that They were all in it together. We were a little vague as to who "They" were but we were certain it was not Us. They were the forces that made sure that in any given situation the rich got richer and the poor got poorer and, more than that, that the scales of justice were short weighted to the advantage of money and power. Life was just one big company store to us, and the prices were not negotiable.

My father was one of the chief proponents of this philosophy, and he never lacked for evidence to support his beliefs. Were high wages considered bad because they made the cost of living go up, but high profits good because they made the stock market go up? Did politicians grow rich on a $20,000-a-year salary? Did the World Series go seven games?

"They're all in it together, kid," he would say.

At an early age I would argue with him: "Dad, they're not all in it together. They couldn't fix a World Series. It just went seven games."

"A long series makes more money than a short series. Figure it out for yourself."

"What about the years when it doesn't go seven games?" I'd ask, triumphantly.

He'd shake his head, unable to believe my naivete. "They do that every once in a while to make it look good and fool nitwits like you. They're all in it together."

That was a long time ago. In the intervening decades I have found that he was indeed right, about the other things if not the World Series.

I only wish he'd lived long enough to experience the 1980s, an era unparalleled in its glorification of the pursuit of wealth—the more undeserved, the better. It was the They're All In It Together Decade. How Ronald Reagan, the emir of wretched excess, would have pleased him; in the manner a disaster pleases the seer who predicted it.

These columns were written in the 1980s and their immediate aftermath; some while in the service of the *Des Moines Register,* the rest for the *Cedar Rapids Gazette.* If they convince you that we do not live in the best of all possible worlds, my life will not have been in vain and my father, wherever he is, will be very happy.

Don't forget, ten copies.

They're All in It Together

❏

1

A MAN FOR ONE SEASON

I MUST CONFESS to being astonished by Ronald Reagan. I first met him in a boys' lavatory while covering the New Hampshire primary in 1980. I walked into a junior high school where he was scheduled to address a rally and was mildly surprised to see my way to the john lined with bright-eyed townspeople wearing expectant, vaguely adulatory looks.

"I hadn't realized they knew about me up here," I said to myself. And, as it turned out, they didn't. I walked into the john to find none other than the Gipper himself, alone, being human. Thank God I wasn't an assassin. We stood at adjoining urinals, doing what was necessary, until I finally broke the silence with: "How's it going, Governor?" (Did I mention I'm not an investigative reporter?)

"Pretty well" he answered. Not exactly Stanley and Livingston, is it? Ah well, you go with the anecdotes you've got.

That was to be the only time I ever spoke to the man, a privation under which I have borne up rather well. I have never forgotten that brush with greatness, however. I only wish I'd thought to ask him to autograph a piece of paper.

I followed him around the state that day, listening to him speak to perhaps seven or eight crowds. He was remarkable. He gave the same speech at every stop, of course, all politicians do; but he was able to do it exactly the same way every time, with the catch in his voice falling on the same syllable and the tears clouding his vision at precisely the same moment.

He talked about a time when respect for the United States was so great in the world that an American citizen could walk through any revolution unharmed, simply by putting a small American flag in his or her lapel. He promised to restore that kind of universal respect. It was utter nonsense, of course, but it went over well in New Hampshire, where the license plates say: "Live Free or Die." It convinced me, however, that his quest for the presidency was doomed.

"The man is a fool or a charlatan," I said. "In either case, the American people will find him out."

Well, to make a long story short, they didn't. I tried to warn them—Lord knows, I tried—but to no avail. This was my warning, issued on the eve of the 1980 election:

"To paraphrase one of his tag lines, where is the rest of him? Ronald Reagan is not merely an ignoramus, he is a man who glories in his ignorance, who wears it as a badge of honor. When he tells us he has not read a book in the past fifteen years or so, he expects us to break into applause. He is a Western American version of the English squire one finds in the novels of Fielding and Trollope—a yokel who takes extraordinary pride in having lived a life uncorrupted by knowledge or serious thought.

"None of which would automatically disqualify him for the presidency—we've had ignorant presidents before—but he appears at a time when the forces of superstition and ignorance are on the rise in our society, and he has become their champion.

"Ronald Reagan is the candidate of the faith-healers, phrenologists, tin-foil collectors, numerologists, astrologers and airport mendicants. Not exclusively, of course. There are intelligent people who against all odds favor Reagan, but they stand out in the Republican ranks like deer in a flock of sheep. While a candidate cannot be held completely responsible for his supporters, neither can he be totally divorced from them, and when I look at Reagan's supporters, I shudder."

Shudder along:

In those early days of the Reagan administration when all things, however absurd, seemed possible, going back to the gold standard was bandied about. So I bandied back:

Cross of Gold, Revisited

When I was a lad, pursuing a college education at a safe distance, I studied economics; macro-economics, micro-economics,

labor economics, Keynesian economics, everything but home economics. You have to draw the line somewhere.

One of the things I was taught was that the gold standard was a
bunch of baloney. It wasn't flexible enough to deal with the needs of
a modern economy, I was told. The only people who believed in it
were people who also thought that the Communists were behind the
fluoridation of drinking water or that the earth was flat—or both.

No more. Suddenly, virtually out of nowhere, the intellectual air
is filled with gold bugs, people who want to go back to the gold standard to save our economy. A number of Reaganomists—Jude (The
Obscure) Wanniski, Arthur (The Curve) Laffer, Alan (The Laugher)
Greenspan—say it's the solution to all of our problems. Whom is one
to believe?

I believe my father.

"They're all in it together," he used to say. That was his philosophy and it never failed him. I can imagine going to him and asking if
he was in favor of going back to the gold standard.

"What for?" he'd snort.

"A lot of President Reagan's advisers are saying it's the only way
to control inflation."

"Oh sure, inflation; I forgot. They're right. I remember the last
time we were on the gold standard. Nineteen thirty-one and thirty-
two. We didn't have any inflation. Of course, we didn't have any jobs
either, but things were cheap."

"The Reagan people say the gold standard had nothing to do with
the Depression. The Depression was caused by the Hawley-Smoot
Tariff, they say."

"That's what all the guys on the bread line thought too. 'Damn
shame about the Hawley-Smoot Tariff,' they'd say. 'If it wasn't for
that, life would be a bowl of cherries.' What a laugh."

"You think the gold standard caused the Depression?"

"What do I look like, an economist? I'll tell you this, though: I
remember when we were on the gold standard. If it was such a good
thing, how come life was so terrible?"

"Terrible?"

"Yes, terrible. Terrible for me and people like me. You had to
work all day, six days a week, just to put food on the table. Kids had

to leave school and take jobs in factories to help their families make ends meet. Farmers had it even worse. The big shots, the bankers, the railroads, owned the country lock, stock and barrel. They plated the faucets in their mansions with gold. That was the gold standard, my boy."

"You can't blame all that on the gold standard, Dad."

"Maybe not. All I know is that it was part of a pattern. Reagan wants to take us back to the good old days—small government, the gold standard, Calvin Coolidge. Let me tell you something: I was there. I don't want to go back. And you don't have to have a fancy college education, like the one I bought for you, to know one thing: If the gold standard was a good thing for working people, for poor people, Reagan wouldn't be for it. He's a rich man's president."

"But the Reagan people say that the ones hurt most by inflation are the poor and the elderly, the ones least able to afford it."

"People least able to afford it are hurt most by almost everything. If Reagan is so interested in the elderly and the poor, he should stop trying to cut hot lunch programs and food stamps."

"You don't think the gold standard is good for anything then?"

"There's nothing that isn't good for somebody. The gold standard is good for somebody, but you and me ain't them. Wake up kid. They're all in it together."

That's what he'd say if he were alive today. It makes sense. (1982)

I am sometimes asked how I, along with a very few other Washington journalists, was able to resist the Reagan charm for so many years (and manage it to this day).

I don't understand the question. What's to resist? If a man comes to your door to sell you an encyclopedia with blank pages, you resist his charm. Mr. Reagan always seemed to me a complete fraud and phony.

He did, however, have an extraordinary ability to ignore reality. This ability did not do much to solve the budget deficit, but on occasion it allowed him to project strength and courage, a valuable attribute for a leader. For example:

"I Don't Have Cancer,
My Nose Does"

President Reagan's reaction to his latest cancer scare is a perfect example of why so many people love him; and why he drives so many of us crazy.

There is an undeniable personal grace about the man. Faced with a health crisis, a polyp on his colon, a bullet in his chest or a skin lesion on his nose, he shrugs it off with a joke and a smile. He has a kind of indomitable optimism about him that is all but indistinguishable from courage. Even his critics, of whom I count myself as one, admire that about him.

But he doesn't understand *anything*. He called the bandage on his nose a "billboard." "Stay out of the sun," was the message, he said.

Yet his administration continues to drag its feet on limiting the production of fluorocarbons, the substance which is thought to destroy the ozone layer above the earth, the depletion of which is thought to increase the risk of skin cancer. His secretary of interior has suggested staying out of the sun as an alternative to doing something about ozone depletion.

The president won't admit that government has a role to play in protecting people even when evidence for the need is as plain as the nose on his face.

He got shot by a nut, but he's against gun control. He's got skin cancer, but he's against the control of fluorocarbons. If there's one thing more indomitable than his optimism, it's his ignorance.

We wish him well, of course. But that bandage on his nose isn't a billboard, it's a wake-up call—and he's sleeping through it. (1987)

To me, for the most part, the Reagan administration was one long march forward, into the past. Come with me now to those days of yesteryear when out of the past come the hoofbeats of the great horse, Deaver; the Great Communicator rides again:

Grand Illusions

President Reagan's State of the Union address Tuesday was a masterpiece of feel-good fantasy wrapped in self-delusion. It picked out the applaud lines from all of his previous campaign speeches and pasted them into a single gooey confection.

"Tonight we look out on a rising America," he said. "The future belongs to the free. We can out-produce, out-compete and out-sell anybody, anywhere in the world. America is on the move!" And that was the controversial part.

The picture the president painted of this country was a comforting one—strong, brave, just, prosperous, happy—a *Saturday Evening Post* cover by Norman Rockwell. Which is all right so far as it goes, but I think we have a right to expect a little more from our chief executive. A touch of reality, perhaps.

And the reality, as a less jolly leader might have told us, is that we are a nation living off past capital and future earnings. We are using up our roads and bridges and sewage systems and libraries and public facilities faster than we are replacing them, and we are purchasing 20 percent of the government we get with a credit card.

There was hardly a suggestion of that in Mr. Reagan's speech. In one breath he yet again railed against government spending, in the next he promised to go forward with the space program, give us more defense, take care of the needy, protect the elderly, support the farmer and guard against catastrophic illness. Oh yes, and cut taxes. I expected Vice-President George Bush, who was sitting behind him, to break into the old Cole Porter tune: "Do do, that voodoo, that you do, so well."

In the budget the president has just submitted to Congress, these are some of the items that go down: training and employment programs, pollution control, conservation, sewage treatment, medical research, child nutrition, energy development. Here are some that go up: military spending, Social Security, Medicaid, civil service retirement programs, military pensions, interest on the deficit.

Notice a pattern in that? We are systematically looting programs that benefit the young and future generations in favor of those that benefit the old or that feed the military.

I'm not one for returning to the days when being old was almost synonymous with being poor (after all, I'm pretty old myself), but I would prefer even that to a future that relegates young people to a life of diminished opportunity.

It was both ironic and characteristic that President Reagan chose to honor children in his State of the Union Address with those four beautiful kids in the balcony, yet proceeds with policies that foreclose the future of children.

"The American dream is a song of hope that rings through the night winter air," President Reagan said. "Vivid, tender music that warms our hearts when the least among us aspire to the greatest things—to venture a daring enterprise; to unearth new beauty in music, literature and art; to discover a new universe inside a tiny silicon chip or a single human cell."

Not even the president really believes that. He's built his career on knowing that the American dream is lower taxes; that and making your kids pay your bills.

If kids want a future, let them tax *their* kids for it. That's the American way. (1986)

Making the Hard Ones
Look Easy

People keep saying that there are no easy solutions to South Africa's problems. Nonsense. There are easy solutions to everything if one has but the wit to see them.

I think that South Africa could go a long way toward quieting unrest and winning world respect with a single bold stroke—electing Ronald Reagan president.

I know what you're going to say: Mr. Reagan is already president of the United States; how can he be president of South Africa? And my answer is: What's to stop him? I don't believe our Constitution prohibits a president from simultaneously serving in that capacity elsewhere. And as for the South African constitution, if there is one, it can hardly be a very fussy document, considering the things that go on over there.

I know what else you're going to say: Mr. Reagan is so busy not dealing with our trade deficit, our budget deficit and the nuclear arms race that he doesn't have time to not deal with South Africa's problems. That ignores Mr. Reagan's genius for governing. He is the first modern American president to govern *exclusively through the making of speeches.* This is a great time-saver. Instead of reading through long files and boring reports, instead of dreary meetings with long-faced cabinet members and bureaucrats, he simply orders up a speech and reads it off. It's the secret of his popularity. Hardly anybody really cares that he doesn't do anything; it's the saying that matters.

So how long can it take to make a couple dozen speeches a year? He could work in being president of South Africa easily. And he'd give great speeches too, not like that Botha, who seems to have learned public speaking from watching World War II Nazi movies. Reagan would go on television and say something like:

"My fellow South Africans. I hope you'll permit me that familiarity. Even though I'm not actually a South African, you've made Nancy and me so welcome here, we feel as though we belong.

"I suppose you've been reading in the paper all week about the so-called riots in Soweto, where 1,100 so-called demonstrators and twelve policemen passed away. It was, of course, a tragedy. Policemen don't grow on trees, which is more than you can say for the rioters, if you know what I mean.

"Ladies and gentlemen, those rioters out there were not true South Africans. They were dedicated Marxist-Leninists intent not on reform, but on destroying this great country and its tradition of minority rights. Is it our fault that black people are a majority?

"I'm probably the only South African president to have headed a labor union, and I've always been for the principle of one man, one vote. But one man, one vote under law. If black people want to get the vote they should work through their elected representatives, as white people do. By flouting the law—staying out after curfew, making public speeches, meeting in groups to discuss forbidden topics— blacks merely demonstrate how unready they are for equality.

"Last week I received a letter from a little twelve-year-old black girl in Soweto. I'd like to share it with you. She wrote: 'Uncle Massa

President Reagan. I have heard in Sunday school that you think to do away with apartheid, our system of democracy here. Oh, please do not do these thing. Do not abandon us. We poor blacks are not yet ready for ruling selves; we need help and guidance from our white brothers. If not for the white man, who would tell us where to dig for gold? Who would tell us where to live? When to go to bed at night? When to get up? We are a happy, simple people who love our slums. Do not take them from us.'

"Well, I just want to say this to that little girl; 'Don't worry about a thing, honey. We are not going to let you fall victim to the oppression of self-determination.'

"You know, when I was governor of California I met one of your greatest soccer players, Ronnie Fuhr. He died tragically, you'll remember, when he choked on a piece of tin foil on a baked potato at a Burbank chophouse. But before he died he told me this: 'Guv, if you ever gets to be president of South Africa and the going gets tough and you don't know how you're going to save apartheid, just tell the lads to win one for the Fuhrer.'

"Well, that's what I'm doing now. I know things look dark out there and racial equality seems just around the corner, but don't give up hope. If we all pull together, we can still win one for the Fuhrer."

I'm telling you, after he made a speech like that there wouldn't be a dry eye in the country, and they'd put his picture on the Krugerand. I think he should go for it; it's selfish of us to keep him all to ourselves. (1985)

I know people say that one of President Reagan's great accomplishments was the rebuilding of our military strength; I know that. I thought it was a stupendous waste of money and nothing—not the collapse of the Evil Empire, the rise of the New Stalinism from its ruins nor the war in the Middle East—has changed my mind.

I am the kind of military thinker who believes that once you're able to kill an enemy three or four times over, that's enough. If you can't discourage him by killing him three times, give up. That's the real lesson of Vietnam.

President Reagan never saw a weapons system he didn't like. Before Star Wars, there was . . .

Dense Pack

I tried to be positive about President Reagan's Dense-Pack plan for basing the MX missile, I really did. I listened with the open mind of a child as the president explained it. After careful consideration, however, I have to say this:

I think it's one of the most idiotic ideas I've ever heard. It is astonishingly, crushingly stupid; the Edsel of nuclear war. If the president had any guts or smarts, he would fire the fellow who suggested the harebrained scheme to him, he would fire the people who suggested it to that fellow, he would fire the people who thought it up in the first place and he would fire the secretaries who typed it up. Then he would have all of their offices fumigated.

And that's as positive as I get about the MX.

Consider the evidence:

One of the premises behind the MX Dense-Pack plan is that you can bury a missile in enough steel and concrete so that only a direct hit from a nuclear bomb will destroy it. There's no proof of that. The Defense Department says: "In mid-1981 the Defense Nuclear Agency reported on a series of tests and analyses to validate silo-hardness levels. The conclusion of that work was that superhard silo designs are feasible. This breakthrough permitted the development of the close-spacing system."

Did you get that word—*breakthrough*? What breakthrough? Saying that you can protect a missile from a nuclear hit doesn't make it so. The only breakthrough is in their heads.

Another premise on which Dense-Pack depends is that the explosions from the first enemy missiles to hit the pack will destroy or knock off target the enemy missiles right behind them. Which is a terrific theory, but nobody knows whether it's true either. When you say it with conviction, however, it sounds true.

For this collection of ifs, maybes and outright ha-has, we are asked to pay a mere $25 billion. If you converted $25 billion into

$10,000 bills and laid them end to end, they would reach anywhere you wanted them to.

Even if Dense-Pack worked, it wouldn't be worth that kind of money. We have, in fact, an invulnerable counter-attack force—our submarine-based missiles. We also have airborne cruise missiles which are relatively invulnerable. Any attack or suggestion of an attack by the Russians would unleash upon them the greatest holocaust ever to befall any nation.

They might have a few missiles left when the mushroom clouds settled, but they wouldn't have a country. Neither would we. Their allies would be destroyed, as would ours. That is the reality of nuclear war. It is not winnable nor, in any meaningful sense, survivable.

We have about 7,500 nuclear warheads aimed at the Russians and their friends. They have about the same number. And each of them makes the Hiroshima and Nagasaki bombs, which killed 200,000 Japanese and wounded 130,000 others, look like Fourth of July firecrackers. The world needs more missiles like John DeLorean needs a tax loss.

I know what you're wondering. You're wondering how come I'm so smart and the president and his pals are so dumb.

I'm not sure, but I can say with confidence that the transparently stupid schemes of the military never seem so to the generals.

In World War I, they kept sending men out of the trenches into machine gun fire, killing hundreds of thousands at a crack. They did that for four years and they never figured out that machine guns can kill faster than men can cut through barbed wire.

The French built the Maginot Line prior to World War II to protect themselves against Germany and, when the time came, the Germans simply went around it.

The generals even tried to build an electronic barrier across Vietnam in the 1960s to keep the North Vietnamese out of the South. It was a dippy idea that never got off the ground, but it was seriously proposed.

This new MX plan is another in a long line of expensive, unworkable, wasteful military fantasies that would be laughable if not so tragic in its consequences. "Peacekeeper," they call it. Dense-Pack.

The real dense pack is that gang in the White House. (1982)

Ollie's Follies

One last word on the appearance of Ollie North before the Iran-Contra panel, before its memory fades:

It was so good it almost made me glad that television was invented. It had passion, humor, pathos, plot, theme and character. It was better than baseball.

North charged into the public consciousness last week trailing intimations of John Wayne and Clark Gable. He was the can-do man of action who could cut through the red tape the whey-faced bureaucrats rolled out by the mile. He was interested in results and, by God, he got them. By last Friday he was a national hero.

That, if polls are to be believed, is the way he seemed to most people. To me, he seemed like Milo Minderbinder.

Minderbinder is, of course, one of the chief characters in Joseph Heller's great comic novel *Catch-22*. He is a lieutenant who parlays his job as a mess officer at a World War II air base in the Mediterranean into a huge, multi-national conglomerate that threatens to take over the conduct of the war. Ever since the Iran-Contra scandal broke I've been impressed with the parallels between Heller's bizarre fictional world and the Reagan White House, but never more than when North was testifying on the Byzantine financial arrangements he made to siphon money off for the Contras.

Listening to him talk about profits that weren't really profits but "residuals" reminded me of Minderbinder describing how he is able to make a four-cent profit on eggs he buys at seven cents, then sells for five.

"I'm the people I buy them from," he says. "I make a profit of three and a quarter cents apiece when I sell them to me and a profit of two and three quarter cents apiece when I buy them back from me. That's a total profit of six cents an egg. I lose only two cents an egg when I sell them to the mess halls, at five cents apiece, and that's how I can make a profit. I pay only one cent apiece at the hen when I buy them in Sicily." Doesn't that sound like North's Iran-Contra scam to you?

Minderbinder eventually expands his operation to include the prosecution of the war. He rents out government planes to the highest bidder. At one point he is contracted by the Americans to bomb a German-held bridge and by the Germans to defend it. He does both. At another point he has his bombers bomb their own base, then strafe it. "We have no choice," he says when he's questioned about it. "It's in the contract." It is the ultimate privatization of foreign policy, different only in degree from our sale of arms to an Iran which we are now threatening to attack.

The *Catch-22* parallels don't stop there. One of the most compelling is the character named Major Major, a hapless Henry Fonda look-alike who is promoted to the rank of major by "an IBM machine with a sense of humor" four days after his enlistment as a private. He is made squadron commander, a responsibility that makes him so miserable that he retreats into isolation. He sits in his office and instructs his executive officer not to let "anyone to come in to see me while I'm here." Is that Ronald Reagan or what? The only people he allows to tell him what's going on are the people who don't know.

And perhaps the clearest expression of the spirit of *Catch-22* in the Reagan White House is delivered by an old Italian woman in the book who says, of soldiers who have driven townspeople from their homes:

"Catch-22 says they have a right to do anything we can't stop them from doing."

The Great Communicator couldn't have said it better himself. (1987)

An Expert Opinion

In the immortal words of Dan Rather, it's time to call in the dogs and put out the fire. Or maybe it's the other way around. In any case, the hunt is over. President Reagan is innocent; he didn't know what was going on. How do I know? Richard Nixon told me so.

Hey! Would Richard Nixon lie?

Mr. Nixon is perhaps the most consistent political analyst we have. No matter how big a jam an American president is in, no matter what the circumstances, his response is the same: The president is not a crook. It's nice to have a theme to one's life.

Adding another chapter to his remarkable rehabilitation, Mr. Nixon addressed a conference of Republican governors last week in a session closed to the press. Closed sessions being what they are, the *Washington Post* printed a partial transcript almost immediately.

Nixon dealt with the crisis President Reagan faces over the Iran-Contra imbroglio.

"It is not going to be another Watergate, as long as you stay ahead of the curve," he said. "You had Colonel North and some others skimming some money off and giving it to the Contras. That was illegal, apparently. But President Reagan didn't know that. I know that because he just wasn't involved in details. He has told me so. I believe him."

Whew! Doesn't that clear up a lot of what you've been worrying about? I particularly like the "*That was illegal, apparently*" line. Vintage Nixon. He also leaves open the question of whether Mr. Reagan told him that he had no knowledge of the skimming or merely that he didn't know it was illegal. The man never lets you down. He is to shifty what Larry Bird is to basketball. (1986)

Speaking of The Richard:

God, I miss Richard Nixon. There was a president you could get your teeth into.

Try writing satire about Ronald Reagan some time. You feel as though you're trying to punch out a giant marshmallow. I mean, how many ways are there to say "amiable dunce"?

But Nixon, ah Nixon . . . there was a piece of work. When you attacked Richard Milhous Nixon you got blood and bones and gristle and fur. You got bitten back. It was fun hating Richard Nixon.

Which is why I love him. Did you see him on television this past week? First on "60 Minutes" last Sunday, then "American Parade" on Tuesday? He was wonderful, at the top of his game.

Villains are almost always more interesting than heroes, and aging villains are the most interesting of all. As a villain grows old and power passes from his hands, his faults tend to become indistinguishable from his virtues. You begin to admire him for the same qualities you used to hate him for. With Nixon, it's that sense of betrayal received and given that animates one's memory of him.

There was a lovely example of it on the show Tuesday. His interviewer asked the former president about an incident that Henry Kissinger had related in his memoirs. It was the one about Nixon, in the last days of his presidency, forcing Kissinger to get on his knees and pray with him in the Lincoln bedroom.

It was an awkward, embarrassing incident as told by Kissinger; it made you feel as though Nixon were on the verge of madness in those final days at the White House—the implication being that Kissinger was holding things together.

Nixon acknowledged the essentials of the story, but the sense of his version was that of a battered, beaten man trying to come to terms with the necessity of having to resign the presidency of the United States. The moment of prayer in the Lincoln bedroom, in the company of a close associate, became a poignant, moving anecdote.

Nixon had sensed Kissinger's embarrassment, he said, and shortly after called his secretary of state to apologize for making him feel uncomfortable and to ask that the incident remain a private one. Kissinger assured him that it had not been embarrassing in the least and that there would be no "leak."

"But of course there was," Nixon told his interviewer. And then he flashed that malevolent smile and, eyes gleaming like those of an animal at the back of a cave, added: "And I wasn't surprised."

It was pure Nixon—the self-pity, the calm detached air, the profound cynicism and the quick thrust to the opponent's midsection with a sharp knife. That little anecdote, along with the look and the smile, told more about Nixon's contempt for the honor of Kissinger than he could have revealed in a chapter of his book. It was beautiful. No one does it better.

There were two qualities—two at least—that set Nixon apart from ordinary men. One was his absolute contempt for law. In his dealings with Congress, in his conduct of the war in Vietnam, even in the computation of his income tax, he tried to get away with everything he could.

The other quality was his unparalleled ability to rise from ashes, to persevere where other, lesser men would be discouraged. It was a quality that followed him into private life. (1984)

One last word on the Prince of Darkness:

Richard (Be It Ever So Humble) Nixon finally found a home in New York last week, and he did it with characteristic irony. After having been thwarted in two attempts to buy into big buildings, he purchased a townhouse on East Sixty-fifth Street.

The irony is that the townhouse was the former home of Judge Learned Hand, perhaps the greatest appellate judge never to serve on the Supreme Court.

To have Richard Nixon, who tried to put G. Harrold Carswell on the Supreme Court, living in the former home of Learned Hand truly boggles the mind. It's as though they sold Lassie to a vivisectionist. (1979)

The Gospel According to the Gipper

When in the Course of human events, it becomes necessary for people to get the Government off of their backs and out of their pockets, and to assume for that Government the lower profile which the Laws of Nature and of Nature's God intended, a decent respect for the opinion of mankind—including authoritarian, but not total-itarian, regimes—requires that they should declare the causes which impel them to the action.

We hold these truths to be self-evident, that all men and many women are created more or less equal and, endowed by their Creator with certain unalienable rights, that among these are Freedom from Communism, Freedom from taxes and the Pursuit of the dollar; rights that women of the right sort choose not to exercise, preferring to raise the children.

That to secure these rights, Governments are instituted among Men, deriving their just powers from the consent of the Rich and Powerful.

That whenever any Form of Government becomes destructive of

these ends, we should give the power back to the states, where the disadvantaged and handicapped have a less effective lobby.

The history of Big Government in America is a history of repeated injuries and usurpations, all having as their object the establishment of an absolute Tyranny. To prove this, let Facts be submitted to a candid world.

Big Government has erected a multitude of New Offices and sent swarms of regulators to harass the Silent Majority and eat out their substance.

It has made us vulnerable to our enemies by allowing our National Defense to deteriorate to the point where we can destroy the Soviet Union only ten times over, while the Russians maintain the capability of destroying us eleven times over.

It has turned its back on our National interest by withholding support from friendly governments which seek to win the loyalty and affection of their citizens through murder and torture.

It has robbed the poor of their incentive to work through such diabolical devices as the Minimum Wage, Compulsory Social Security, Food Stamps and Free School Lunches.

It has pursued a policy of No-growth Socialism that has made a wilderness of many potential strip mines and dimmed the glowing promise of our nuclear energy industry. It has persisted in this foolish effort to conserve our natural resources despite the clear message of the Scriptures that we all will be called to Judgment long before we run out of things to eat.

It has obstructed the Administration of Justice through the appointment of Judges who hold the first Ten Amendments to the Constitution higher than the Ten Commandments.

It has attempted to press upon an unwilling public the notion that guns kill people, when statistics show that, more often than not, they merely wound them.

It has, through its indiscriminate use of the Voting Rights Act, denied the right of Southern office-holders to be elected by the voters of their choice.

It has interfered with the God-given rights of babies in under-developed countries to have equal access to infant formula, regardless of the contamination of the water that is mixed with it.

It has shackled the productivity of the American worker, in the name of Secular Humanism, by interposing itself between the worker and Brown Lung Disease.

It has promoted the breakup of the home and the family by sponsoring programs of sex education for adolescents who would otherwise never figure out where babies come from.

A Government whose character is thus marked by every act which may define a Tyranny is unfit to be the instrument of a Free People.

We, therefore, members of an Evermore Moral Majority, appealing to the Supreme Judge of the world for the rectitude of our intentions, do, in the Name and by the Authority of the good People of These United States, solemnly publish and declare our intention to lower taxes, arm ourselves to the teeth and Unleash Chiang Kai-shek, wherever he may be. (1981)

But Does He Sleep in the Nude?

Back when I was a boy—before television, thank God—there were movie magazines. They had names like *Modern Screen* and *Silver Screen,* and they constituted a distinct literary form—part fiction, part biography, all mush.

They chronicled the lives of Hollywood movie stars, with reality air-brushed out. All the stars, it seemed, lived exemplary lives: courageous and reverent, generous and happy, free of insecurity. Some of the pieces were presented as first-person accounts of Hollywood life.

Those magazines are either dead or changed beyond recognition, but I'm happy to report that the genre is alive and well. It lives on in the soon-to-be-published memoir of Ronald Reagan, excerpted this week in *Time* magazine.

How can a man who can't remember anything write a memoir, you ask? Easy. He hires someone to remember for him, in this case a journalist named Robert Lindsey. The result is a gush of a book worthy of *Modern Screen* at its zenith.

The first excerpt begins:

"Nancy and I awoke early on the morning of November 19,

1985, and at the first glimmer of daylight we looked out from our bedroom at the long, gray expanse of Lake Geneva. There were patches of snow along the edge of the lake and in the gardens of Maison de Saussure, the magnificent, lake-side, eighteenth-century residence that had been lent to us by Prince Karim, the Aga Khan. In the distance we could see the majestic peaks of the Alps."

We're talking here about a man who needs cue cards to talk in his sleep, a man whose grandchildren have to wear name tags to the family Christmas party. Are we to believe he knows the name of the Aga Khan and the century in which his house was built? It's more likely that he thinks the Alps are where Alpo dog food is made.

The bulk of the first installment of this book, called *An American Life,* deals with Mr. Reagan's relationship with Soviet leader Mikhail Gorbachev. To hear him tell it, it was not unlike Errol Flynn's relationship with the evil Burgundians. ("Ten Frenchmen to one Englishman? Those are about the right odds.")

In meeting after meeting Mr. Reagan reveals a lucidity and logic that he hid from us in his public press conferences. By the end of the piece, Gorbachev is reduced to worshipful acquiescence in Mr. Reagan's vision of the world. Clarence Darrow should have been so swift.

If *An American Life* were a real book, one could criticize it for being gruesomely dull, a mish-mash of leftover personal anecdotes that have been warmed over and over in the ovens of White House speech writers and of inside stories of events that have long since been turned inside out. But it is not a real book, it is movie magazine journalism: part fiction, part biography; all mush.

Had I been shopping for a ghost to write Mr. Reagan's book, I would have chosen Jerzy Kosinski. Twenty years ago Kosinski, a Polish emigre, wrote *Being There,* a novel that prefigured the Reagan years to an almost frightening degree.

It is the story of a young man of primitive intelligence who grows up in the house of a mysterious patron who, at the beginning of the book, dies. The young man, named Chance, has spent his life working in the garden and watching television. That's all he's done; that's all he knows.

He is cast out into the street by the executors of the man's will and, through an accident, comes into contact with another rich, sick, powerful old man, who takes a liking to him.

Chance, in his addled way, answers all questions with references to gardening, which the old man takes to be metaphorical. "What do you think of the bad season on the Street?" the old man asks. Chance replies:

"In a garden, growth has its season. There are spring and summer, but there are also fall and winter. And then spring and summer again. As long as the roots are not severed, all is well and all will be well."

The old man is stunned by the profundity of the comment. "What you've just said is one of the most refreshing and optimistic statements I've heard in a very, very long time," he says. Through the old man Chance meets the president of the United States, who is similarly taken by Chance's gardening clichs. And when Chance gets on television with them, he is an instant media sensation. By the end of the book he is being considered for vice-president.

That is as far as Kosinski dared go. In 1970 not even he could envision Chance the gardener being *elected* president.

But he was. And now he's written, more or less, an autobiography, kind of.

Don't you sometimes think we're carrying this life-imitates-art thing too far? (1990)

And at last, at Thanksgiving 1984, a hero:

A Touch of Class

I don't know what you were thankful for yesterday; good health, I hope; true friends, a loving family, enough acorns to get you through the winter. That's what I was thankful for.

But I also gave thanks for George Aiken, for his having been a United States senator for so much of my life. All of us should be thankful for him; we owe him a lot.

Aiken died Monday. They said it was a stroke, but it seems to me that at ninety-two, you die of old age. He was, in every way, a remarkable man and one of the great Americans of his time.

During the thirty-four years the Vermont Republican served in the Senate, he had a hand on virtually every piece of progressive farm legislation that came into law.

A farmer himself, he was an early and effective champion of rural electrification, flood control, federal crop insurance, distribution of food surpluses to the poor and the food stamp program. (It is yet another irony of the Reagan years that the president has convinced people, including farmers, that food stamps are basically a welfare boondoggle for the urban lazy, when the major impetus behind them was farm support.)

But Aiken was more than a farm senator. He was a moving force behind the creation of the St. Lawrence Seaway, a supporter of the great civil rights legislation of the 1960s and, before that, one of the few politicians who stood up to Senator Joseph McCarthy.

To the degree he became nationally famous, it was for something that he never said of the war in Vietnam: "We should declare victory and get out."

What he actually said was that the United States should lessen its commitment gradually until a pullout was possible, but the simplified version was his badge of recognition in his late years.

Truly though, it was his character, his integrity, that made him stand out from his contemporaries. He habitually returned the unused portion of his annual office allowance to the Treasury. He once cast the only vote against adoption of a code of ethics for the Senate because it was too lenient.

And he wore no man's collar. For his last, and successful, re-election campaign in 1968, he listed total expenses of $17.09, most of it for postage on thank-you notes to constituents who had circulated nominating petitions.

He was the last of a vanished breed, men who simply offered themselves for election on the theory that their friends and neighbors knew who they were and what they stood for and could make up their minds without being subjected to a lot of advertising and bragging.

He loved his native state and, unlike most longtime Washington politicians, he went back home when he left office.

"I'm a Vermonter," he said. "I was in prison for thirty-four years and it was time to go free."

I'm not sure even Aiken could be Aiken today. The public now demands that a politician kick, scratch, bite, lie and steal for public office. If he doesn't do that, he doesn't make it through the primary.

Aiken himself was somewhat disillusioned with the process by the time of his retirement. In his autobiography, *Aiken: Senate Diary,* published in 1976, he wrote:

"I have never seen so many incompetent persons in high office. Politics and legislation have become more mixed and smellier than ever."

Plain-spoken, he once said:

"Hell, I'm not religious. My religion is sitting out in the woods on a stump. You can learn a lot there."

His formal education never went beyond high school, but he must have spent a lot of time sitting on stumps in the woods. He knew a lot.

For men like George Aiken, let us be thankful. (1984)

2

THE BUSH THING

I'LL SAY THIS for myself; I never underestimated George Bush. I always knew that beneath that amiable, wimpish exterior was a mean-spirited pettiness that would carry him to the top, or near it.

He had help, of course; chiefly, Mike Dukakis. Mr. Dukakis' campaign was so inept as to suggest sabotage, and he the saboteur. I remember my liberal friends all that summer and fall playing the "Why doesn't he . . . ?" game. Why didn't he defend liberalism, the ACLU, free speech, anything? That's what we wanted to know.

We never found out.

As I write this, Dukakis, having been all but stoned from the state house in Massachusetts, is considering running for the Democratic nomination in 1992, as is George McGovern. Say what you will of the Democrats, they're always good for a laugh. Hopeless, but good for a laugh.

I think George Bush's choice of Dan Quayle as his running mate— incomprehensible at the time—was merely an arrogant act of supreme confidence, like riding a bicycle in traffic with no hands. Or having your horse elected to the Roman senate.

I never overestimated him, either.

Before the Conventions

It looks as though Vice-President George Bush is hip-deep in the doo-doo and sinking fast. He not only is trailing Democrat Michael Dukakis in the polls, he's behind Mikhail Gorbachev. The other day, President Reagan gave his vice-president an endorsement so lacking in warmth that he had to run it through the microwave to get it to room temperature. Each week brings new revelations that cast doubt on his claims that he was innocent of guilty knowledge in either the Iran-Contra follies or the CIA's "Just Say Yes to Noriega" policy. And, for dessert, there is Attorney General Edwin Meese, who seems intent on doing for the Republican Party what Jimmy Hoffa did for the Teamsters. Mother of mercy! Can this be the end of little Georgie?

Don't bet on it.

If Mr. Bush has proved nothing else in his successful primary campaign, it is that he is an adroit campaigner; moreover—and he hasn't gotten the credit he deserves for this—one with a mean streak. When it comes to hardball politics, Preppy George can gouge an eye with the best of them, then complain about his opponent bleeding on his suit.

Senator Robert Dole is the candidate who went into the primaries with a reputation for mean. He was the hombre in the black hat, the one mothers pulled their children off the street for when he'd walk past the house. George Bush left him for dead in New Hampshire.

Before Dole knew what had hit him, he'd been branded a high taxer, a traitor to President Reagan's cause and a fair weather conservative. None of which was true, but it sold well in the no-tax, Reaganite state of New Hampshire. Bush won in a last-minute rush to set himself on the road to the nomination. To add insult to injury, when the bitter Dole confronted Bush with the admonition "Stop lying about my record," he got blamed for being a bad sport.

Bush did somewhat the same thing to Pierre DuPont. DuPont raised altogether legitimate questions about the ultimate solvency of our social security system, questions which Bush dismissed in a debate as "nutty." The crack made Bush look tough and DuPont foolish and helped put to rest Bush's wimp image, but it didn't address the questions.

Running against Bush, Mike Dukakis will find himself attacked in places where he didn't know he had places. The "Massachusetts Miracle" will be made to look like a triumph of Reaganomics, and Dukakis will be painted as a tax-tax-spend-spend Democrat who is salivating to get his hands on the U.S. Treasury.

Bush has some other things going for him too; money, for example. Money isn't everything in politics, but it beats whatever it is that's second-best, and Bush has a lot of it.

He also stands a good chance of basking in the reflected glory of a successful U.S.-Soviet summit, as well as a generally prosperous economy. If you have to run on a platform, "Peace and Prosperity" is the one with the nice ring to it.

His message will be: "We've got a good thing going here; don't let the Democrats screw it up." He might be able to peddle that.

Should the stock market do another October El Foldo, however, the outlook would change. "Peace and Panic" has no ring to it at all. In addition, Mr. Bush is a bit of a drip. He has a way of saying foolish things that make him look like a rich kid trying to be one of the boys or, worse, a member of the ruling class slumming.

His comments at Garfield High School in East Los Angeles last week are a case in point. The predominantly Hispanic school, on which the film "Stand and Deliver" is based, is a minority success story, renown for sending 70 percent of its graduates on to college. Bush went before these upwardly aimed kids and said:

"Even though we emphasize the value of higher learning, you don't have to go to college to be a success. We need the people who build our buildings, who send them soaring into the sky. We need the people who run the offices, the people who do the hard physical work in our society."

That is to inspirational speaking what Elizabeth Taylor is to marriage counseling.

Dukakis is looking good right now, but he has some surprises in front of him. Like real Republicans, for example. Dukakis is from Massachusetts, a state that voted for George McGovern! Conservatives there are Democrats who don't like school busing. Wait until he gets out there among voters who think that the New Deal was a sell-out to the forces of evil or that it is every red-blooded American's duty to own a gun and to shoot someone occasionally. Then we'll see how cool he is.

Don't give up yet, loyal Republicans. George Bush shall rise again. (1988)

After the Conventions

Mike Dukakis took a real beating last week. He got hit over the head with the Pledge of Allegiance and pistol-whipped by handgun control; he was mauled by the drug issue and harpooned by abortion. Those Democrats really know how to hurt a guy.

No, Governor Dukakis was not the victim of Vice-President Bush this time, although he took a few nicks from that quarter too; he got mugged by Congress—the "Democrat-controlled Congress," as the Republicans are fond of saying.

In what amounted to a total repudiation of their chosen candidate, a goodly number of House Democrats banded together with their Republican brethren and did the following:

• Agreed to have the Pledge of Allegiance recited twice a week before opening sessions of the House.

• Voted the death penalty for persons who kill during drug-related felonies.

• Saw the Senate acquiesce to the House's bill denying federal funding for abortions to women made pregnant by rape or incest.

• Voted down a tepid gun control law that would have imposed a seven-day waiting period on handgun purchases.

All of that, in case you haven't noticed, is part of the Bush agenda, none of it favored by Dukakis. Which brings us to the question of the hour:

Why should we, the people of the United States, vote for Michael Dukakis when not even his comrades-in-arms believe in what he stands for? If we're going to have ridiculous drug laws, an absurdist attitude toward guns and an abortion policy that borders on the obscene, as well as debase the flag by wearing it, why not have George Bush as president of the United States? They're his policies, why not give him a chance to execute them?

It seems more and more likely that he'll get that chance. The first presidential debate is being held tonight. The Dukakis people are all atwitter. They think their man, "the best debater in America," is going to cream Bush. Don't count on it.

Bush is easy to underrate. He can look foolish at times and he can be whiny and grating at others, but he has a way of rising to the occasion and he has the best people in the business—the business of mind manipulation—on his team, while the Dukakis bunch is decidedly second-rate.

That speaks well of Dukakis, actually. It says that he is the less Orwellian of the two candidates. He has little talent for demagogy and he is not putty to his handlers. But it speaks *sotto voce,* in a whisper. What speaks loudly to the American people is George Bush standing before the American flag and saying that he is ready to be our leader.

To a remarkable degree the Republicans have controlled the imagery and symbolism of this campaign. They did that in 1980 and 1984, but we cynics discounted it because their flag-carrier was a movie star who was accustomed to following stage directions. The fact that they can do the same thing with a second-banana like George Bush bespeaks an expertise that is breath-taking.

It seems to be working. The other day the *New York Times* published a short series of interviews with voters who had been for Dukakis just after the Democratic convention but who had, in the weeks following, changed their minds. One said:

"When you called me on the poll, I was strongly for Dukakis, based on his convention acceptance speech. But I've reneged on my support for him. I don't go along with his stands on the Pledge of Allegiance, abortion, drugs and prison release. I've completely changed my mind."

Another said: "I was first for Dukakis because everything he was saying was very positive about the women's movement, and he has liberal views about abortion. And I was feeling that since he was the Democrat, he would help the little people, feel and act kindly to the working people.

"But I've been reading newspapers much more in the last month and talking with my husband and friends. To us, Bush seems to be a much stronger person to actually run the country. Our present government, we have been doing well economically and abroad. I figure, you get another person in there, something bad might happen to upset that equilibrium. Maybe we should stick with what we've got."

There were nine interviews presented, all in that vein. While statistically meaningless, they sound an ominous warning to the

Dukakis camp. Those are precisely the kind of people Dukakis needs to convince—and he is unconvincing them.

Perhaps we underestimate the man; perhaps he deliberately has held his fire these many weeks and will unleash the full fury of his intellect on Mr. Bush Sunday, reducing the Vice-President to broken sobs. It's a possibility.

Like Iowa beating UCLA in the Rose Bowl is a possibility. (1988)

UCLA—45, Iowa—28. I don't get enough credit for being right all the time.

Jack Kennedy, Hell
He's Not Even Gerald Ford

The Republicans tried their best to put a happy face on Dan Quayle's performance in the vice-presidential debate last week—they were quick to point out that he hadn't liberated Poland or called Mexico the capital of China—but, let's face it folks, he was awful.

From the opening bell he looked like a scared rookie playing in a league two levels above his competence. It was almost painful to watch as he struggled with each question, searching his memory bank for the index card with the answer his handlers had provided him. Sometimes he found it; very often he didn't.

Questioned about his consistent record of voting against programs that provide nutrition and health care for children of the poor, he said:

"What we have done for the poor is that we, in fact, the homeless bill, the McKinney Act, which is a major piece of legislation that deals with homeless. The Congress has cut the funding that the administration recommended. And the poor and poverty. The biggest thing that we have done for poverty in America is the Tax Simplification Act of 1986. Six million working poor families got off the payroll. Six million people are off the tax-paying payrolls because of that tax reform, and they're keeping the tax money there."

I suppose there's an answer in there somewhere. The problem is that it's the wrong answer. Trying to explain how he would use the military to help stop drug trafficking, he said:

"And there's another thing that will be more important than the premise of this question on a hypothetical of using troops. We'll use military assets. We're not going to, we will use military assets, but we need to focus on another part of the problem."

Like syntax, perhaps. Senator Quayle speaks English as though it were his second language, with his first language being sign. He makes Tarzan sound glib. George Bush is inarticulate; Dan Quayle is incoherent.

He might have teetered through the evening without suffering a mortal wound, however, had it not been for the pesky persistence of Tom Brokaw. Brit Hume had already twice asked Quayle what he would do if the presidency were suddenly thrust upon him, and Quayle had been unable to come up with a satisfactory answer. He'd pray, he said. He'd "traveled a number of times," he knew Margaret Thatcher. They were strange responses, actually, because the question is in the nature of a softball. All you have to do is think continuity, and the steps a new president must take to reassure the nation, our allies and our enemies that a firm new hand is on the tiller become fairly obvious. Apparently Mr. Quayle's continuity answer was stuck behind his contra-aid card; anyway, he couldn't get it out.

Still, it was remarkable that Brokaw thought to bring up the subject yet again and give Quayle one last swing at it. This time Quayle made the mistake of playing his Jack Kennedy card, something he does freely on the stump. "I have as much experience in the Congress as Jack Kennedy did when he sought the presidency," he said.

Bentsen was ready for that. It was almost poetry.

"Senator," he said, "I served with Jack Kennedy. I knew Jack Kennedy. Jack Kennedy was a friend of mine.

"Senator, you're no Jack Kennedy."

Pow! Right in the kisser. If the debate had been a prizefight they wouldn't have had to stop it, they could have counted Quayle out right there.

Even allowing for the possibility that the response was scripted, it didn't sound scripted. In a debate in which it was transparently evident that both candidates were giving canned responses again and again, it came across as a moment of genuine passion, a friend rising in outrage to the defense of a martyred comrade's memory.

In the context of the evening it reinforced the image of Quayle as a pip-squeak trying to play with the big guys, but not succeeding.

There is something unattractively young about Senator Quayle; not boyishness, but childishness. Asked what experience had shaped his political philosophy, the best he could produce was his grandmother's advice: "You can do anything you want to, if you just set your mind to it and go to work."

That's a nice enough thought. Of course, it carries more weight when grandma is a millionaire. As if Quayle's position in life had anything to do with hard work.

None of which means that Dan Quayle will not be vice-president of the United States. Vice-presidential debates are not crucial to campaigns, but this one was more important than most, and the Republicans were big losers.

What it really means is that for many of us the prospect of a Bush-Quayle victory has gone from alarming to terrifying. (1988)

Call in the Dogs, Dan

Even though it ain't over till it's over, sometimes it's so close to being over that it might as well be. Goodbye Dukakis, hello President Bush.

If the debate Thursday was supposed to resuscitate Mike Dukakis' wilting presidential hopes, it failed. George Bush, I thought, turned him every way but loose. He was firm without being nasty, affable without being silly and confident without being smug. He was, in short, the best possible George Bush.

Not that Dukakis was so terrible; he was just . . . well . . . Dukakis. His main job in this debate was to demonstrate that he was not the heartless technocrat that some believe him to be, that he was a creature of blood and bile and emotion, just like the rest of us. The very first question did him in.

He was asked something to the effect: "If you came home one night to find your wife raped and murdered, your mother hanging on a meat hook and your dog fed into your snow blower, would you get mad?"

"No," Dukakis said. "I would call 812, the police emergency number my administration installed and which has reduced crime in the greater Massachusetts area by 9.5 percent. When the police apprehended the person who did it, I would make sure that they did not put the handcuffs on too tight or speak rudely to him, lest they violate his civil rights." Or words to that effect.

The problem with Dukakis is that he thinks being human is a weakness, which is fine if you're a parking meter. But if you're running for president it's best to show you share some human frailties with the people you seek to lead.

Dukakis showed the same lack of the common touch—or any touch, for that matter—when asked to name his contemporary heroes. "Joe DiMaggio," he might have said, then lowered the eyebrows of the audience as he explained his theory of "class" and how DiMag epitomized it. He could have named any number of working-class heroes; instead, he ran off a list of occupations—cops, politicians, teachers, preachers. He sounded more like he was running for guidance counselor than president. Bush, meanwhile, was picking a hero from every voting bloc he needed to win, ending with a paean to President Reagan. At that point, the liberals in the room where I was watching the debate covered their eyes. We were afraid Bush would break out his straw hat and cane and do a cake walk across the stage singing "If you lika me, like I lika you."

Oh well, one thing you have to say for us liberals: we know how to lose with grace. It comes with practice. I suppose we should start getting our affairs in order, preparing ourselves for the Bush(ugh)-Quayle administration.

It's Quayle who makes it hard. I could live with George Bush; there are even those who say he's a decent man, although you wouldn't know it from the campaign he's run. But why did he have to give us Dan Quayle, a baby-faced, right-wing ideologue with the intellectual acuity of a geranium? I remember when, in a similar situation, Dwight Eisenhower raised the young Richard Nixon out of the mud and into our political life. He was there for the next twenty-five years. I fear we can expect no less from Dan Quayle. How could Bush have pulled such a dirty trick on us? Is it his idea of a practical joke, or what?

The other thing that makes Bush a particularly bitter pill is his relentless attack on Dukakis' membership in the American Civil Liberties Union. It smacks of the Southern politician who accused his opponent of being monogamous, even though married.

The strategy depends for its effectiveness on ignorant prejudice and, in depending on it, reinforces it. Bush knows that the ACLU isn't *for* criminals and communists simply because it defends them in cases. The group has also defended Nazis and John Birchers and anti-abortionists and Young Americans for Freedom, as well as Ollie North. It's the rights of these people that the ACLU defends and, with them, our rights. Bush knows that. His father, Prescott Bush, was one of the senators who led the censure of Joe McCarthy in the Senate. To act as Bush has acted shames his heritage.

Moderate Republicans (I would say liberal Republicans, but I don't want anyone to swoon with shame) have always considered Bush one of their own. They are as dismayed as the rest of us at the campaign he has waged, but they expect a return to his former self once he's in office.

There's a saying in sports: You play like you practice. In politics, you govern as you campaign. George Bush will take office with a mandate for nothing except leading the nation in the Pledge of Allegiance.

For this we needed an eighteen-month campaign? (1988)

Bush Wins,
Offers Olive Branch

So *now* he wants to be president of all the people; *now* he wants to bind up wounds, unite us all for the common good and play kissy-face with his enemies. Now that George Bush has won, he wants to let bygones be bygones.

Sorry Genghis, my dance card is full.

I am one of those people known as a sore loser. Oh, I don't mind losing an election—Lord knows, I've lost enough of them—but when a candidate burns an "L" on my lawn, plays up to the Yahoo vote and tells egregious lies about my team, I am not going to rush to his embrace just because his appalling tactics proved successful. So I am unmoved when Mr. Bush calls me to his kinder, gentler America.

Mike Dukakis doesn't feel that way, apparently. Appearing just after the election—his ear hanging by a thread and his nose pushed around to the side of his head by the mugging Bush had administered to him—Dukakis said of Mr. Bush: "He will be our president. And we will work with him."

You always were a wimp, Mike. That's why you lost.

Personally, I am not going to work with President Bush. Why should I? I'm a liberal, someone way out of the mainstream. I believe in social justice, civil rights. I am even a card-carrying member of the ACLU (or would be if I paid my dues). Why would Mr. Bush want the support of such a degenerate, anyway? I might be harboring a fugitive murderer-rapist in my attic, I might celebrate the Fourth of July by burning the flag. You never know with liberals.

No, Mr. President-elect, you're better off without me. I shall continue to stand at the side of the battle, making faces and rude noises.

I would, however, offer this advice to those Democrats and liberals who would co-operate with the next president: "Don't let him raise taxes."

I know, we're going to need a tax rise sooner or later to save the country; it doesn't matter. You've had this game played on you before. Ronald Reagan was elected on a promise not to raise taxes, then he raised them and blamed the Democrats. Don't let Bush do the same thing!

If President Bush finds that he can't get along without new taxes, make him go to the American people and say: "Remember when I said I wouldn't ever raise taxes? Read my lips—I lied." If the country needs saving, let George take the fall. It's either that or reconciling yourselves to never again having a liberal in the White House.

In any case, an argument could be made that Mr. Bush has a clear mandate from the American people to run enormous budget deficits. Surely there was no indication that they were unhappy in the slightest with the huge deficits run up by the Reagan administration. And Mr. Bush's campaign promises to lower taxes and raise defense spending—a certain prescription for even higher deficits—brought no howls of outrage from voters. There you have it. The American people want a big deficit. Congress should help President Bush achieve it. We are a democracy, after all.

If you infer from the foregoing that I am a tad bitter about the recent election, you are right. I felt that Mr. Bush ran a truly reprehensible campaign, and I took it personally.

I didn't mind its overall negativeness—I rather like negative campaigns, saying bad things about your opponent has a certain air of sincerity about it—but several times it reached beyond that into dangerous and destructive demagogy. The first instance was when the campaign used President Reagan to promote a rumor that Dukakis had undergone psychiatric treatment earlier in his life. The campaign denied that it had anything to do with the rumor, but I discount that. You don't get a vicious rumor broadcast from the mouth of the president without some planning.

In any case, what the episode did was reinforce the notion that there is a stigma attached to seeking professional help in times of great stress, something that set the cause of mental health back twenty years. And they used the office of the presidency to do it. That was low.

Then there were the Willie Horton ads, featuring pictures of the black man who had committed a rape while on furlough from his prison term for murder. The Bush people said the ad had nothing to do with race, but that's absurd. You simply can't show a black thug like that, night after night, without exciting racial stereotypes, in this case the black guy who wants to rape your sister.

It was dirty, rotten, segregationist campaigning, and it was unforgivable.

And now, all of a sudden, Bush wants to be Mr. Nice Guy.

Sorry Mr. President-elect. With a courtship like you gave us, who needs a honeymoon? We'll go straight to the fighting. (1988)

An Oyster Bay Kind of Guy

At long last, we know what George Bush wants to be when he grows up. Teddy Roosevelt.

At least that's what he indicated the other day. "I'm an Oyster Bay kind of guy," he said. "Maybe I'll turn out to be a Teddy Roosevelt."

Sure. And maybe I'll turn out to be Anastasia's grandson, heir to the Russian throne.

True, there are certain similarities between Mr. Bush and T.R. Both were rich kids. Both Republicans. Both members of big families.

And . . . that's it.

Teddy Roosevelt came to influence just as the nation was trying on the vestments of a world power for the first time. We were then a muscular, rambunctious nation, confident and optimistic. Teddy Roosevelt embodied that spirit. He was at once an idealist, a ruthless pragmatist and, above all, a bully preacher in the bully pulpit.

George Bush takes office at a time less ripe with possibility. Having conquered the century, we are a nation sliding steadily into decline, content to take our prosperity at the expense of the future. The optimism which once fueled our accomplishments is now used to artificially brighten a dim future. We are a great power trying to hang on to its greatness for just a few more years. That is the spirit embodied by George Bush.

It is as preacher, however, that the analogy between Roosevelt and President Bush is most ludicrous. This is Teddy Roosevelt in 1899, speaking on public service:

"Far better it is to dare mighty things, to win glorious triumphs, even though checkered by failure, than to take rank with those poor spirits who neither enjoy much nor suffer much, because they live in the gray twilight that knows not victory nor defeat."

This is George Bush, speaking last week to an inner city youth who asked him how he, the president, keeps drugs out of his life:

"Keep them out of your life? Well, kind of getting along in my level of life here, the pressures aren't quite that big. You don't have a lot of guys coming up to you in daily life saying, 'Hey.' So I don't have the temptations and the pressures that you've got like young guys in school and all of that.

"Now, like, I'm president. It would be pretty hard for some drug guy to come into the White House and start offering it up, you know? But I bet if they did, I hope I would say, 'Hey, get lost. We don't want any of that.''

What we're talking about here, friends, is an eloquence gap. Roosevelt strapped wings to an idea and sent it soaring; Bush feeds it mush until it gets tired and goes away.

No, this is not going to be a Teddy Roosevelt presidency. It's going to be a Mr. Rogers presidency. You remember Fred Rogers of the children's television show? He'd come in the door, hang up his coat in the closet and sing: "It's a beautiful day in the neighborhood, it's a beautiful day in the neighborhood, won't you be my friend?" Then, at the close of the show, he'd say: "I like you just the way you are."

That's George Bush, more or less. Paul Weyrich, the professional right wing nut, savages John Tower, Mr. Bush's choice for defense secretary, and Mr. Bush sends him a thank-you note. Congress clamps handcuffs on his ability to conduct policy in Central America, he smiles and says isn't bipartisanship wonderful. Exxon mucks up one of the world's most beautiful shorelines and he says it could have been worse.

Bush is not only kinder and gentler, he is insipid.

Personally, I prefer my presidents with larger virtues and darker faults. Richard Nixon, for example. A recent biography of Sam Goldwyn, the movie pioneer, has produced yet another great Nixon anecdote.

Nixon, in search of Hollywood support for his upcoming 1972 re-election campaign, decided to award Goldwyn, then ninety, the Medal of Freedom.

In making the award he gave a canned speech, similar to one he'd given in honor of Walt Disney shortly before. The feeble Goldwyn nodded, then tugged at the president's coat. Nixon leaned close to the old man's lips, and Goldwyn said: "You'll have to do better than that if you want to carry California."

The president straightened abruptly and closed the ceremony. On the way out the president asked Goldwyn's son, Sam Junior, whether he'd heard what his father had said. Junior, who had, said he hadn't.

Nixon brightened: "He said, 'I want you to go out and beat those bastards.'"

That may not be eloquence but it's something. Why can't we have presidents like Richard Nixon anymore? (1989)

No, Virginia

Around the holiday season columnists get letters from children asking guidance. Trapped between the innocence of youth and the cynicism of the times, they are confused as to what is real and what is fantasy, and they ask our advice. I got such a letter the other day.

"Dear Columnist," it began, "I am an eight-year-old girl in Parched Throat, Texas, and I read you all the time. My parents tell me I should be reading something to improve my mind but I don't care, I like you. I need your help.

"Yesterday I overheard my father tell my mother that he didn't believe in George Bush. I didn't understand, because it was just after a man on television calling himself George Bush said he was invading Panama for its own good. He looked real to me.

"Tell me, sir, is there a George Bush?—(signed) Virginia S."

I wrote her back:

"Dear Virginia—No George Bush? Well, I'm sorry to be the one to break the news to you, kid, but your father is right.

"The fact that you see someone called George Bush on television doesn't mean anything, any more than the Santa Claus you see in every department store means anything. They can do wonders with makeup these days.

"You have to ask yourself this; if there were a George Bush—a kinder, gentler man who liked puppies and children—would he have sent a delegation to China to embrace the butchers of Tiananmen Square? Would he have vetoed a bill to extend the student visas of the young Chinese who attracted the hostile attention of their government by engaging in protests against the massacre of their comrades back home? And would he have done it just as Chinese authorities were announcing an intensified campaign to find and punish last summer's protesters? I don't think so.

"Remember those pictures from Beijing on your television last June? Remember that lonely figure in the white shirt who faced down the column of tanks? How thrilled we all were by his courage. The American mission to Beijing sold that fellow out, along with all those hundreds of unarmed students who were gunned down by government troops. What we, as the last best hope of Mankind, said loud and clear to those students and their surviving colleagues was: 'We don't care.' The George Bush we've heard about, a deeply compassionate man who loves the American flag and the Pledge of Allegiance, wouldn't have done that.

"Oh, I know, you can argue that China is an important country and we have to keep on good terms with it. It seems kind of dumb, though, to throw your hand in with the eighty-year-old despots who run the country now, and against the generation of future leaders. It kind of reminds you of when we backed the Shah of Iran because he was our kind of tyrant.

"And then there's the murder of those priests in El Salvador. We brought the only known witness to the United States and, according to her, subjected her to relentless interrogation, as though she were the criminal. We invited the Salvadoran military in to bully her, to threaten her with deportation unless she changed her story of having seen government troops commit the murders. Then, when she changed her story, we gave her a lie detector test, which she flunked and we announced that she was an unreliable witness.

"Would George Bush do an absolutely swinish thing like that simply to protect the credibility of his destitute policy in Central America? Wash your mouth out with soap, Virg; this is an American president we're talking about.

"The government has denied the woman's allegation, of course, just as it denied the accusation of an American human rights worker in El Salvador who said she'd been tortured by Salvadoran troops while an American embassy official was present. We said she was lying because American officials simply don't do things like that. Don't you think if there were a George Bush, a Yale man, our denials would be more persuasive?

"I'm sorry Virginia. Ask me whether there's a Santa, why don't you? I can give you a maybe. But a George Bush? No way.—Your friend, the Columnist." (1989)

More Mush from the Wimp

I've heard some cynical speeches in my time—there was Richard Nixon's "I Am Not a Crook" effort and Lyndon Johnson on the Gulf of Tonkin incident—but I don't believe I've ever heard a president give a more blatherous account of himself than George Bush did Tuesday in his televised address to Congress.

It was majestic in its insincerity, underwhelming in its vacuousness. It was unctuous, pandering and base. Naturally, it was a big hit.

The American people love blather. I think it reinforces the superstition that life is a television commercial. The only time an American politician gets into trouble is when he blurts out the truth, as when he suggests that government must be paid for by taxes. So long as he sticks to sweet-sounding insincerity he's safe. That was the secret of Ronald Reagan's great success and young George studied well at the knee of the master.

Bush's blather came in two flavors Tuesday: foreign and domestic. First the foreign:

He said that our Persian Gulf intervention had been made in the service of a new world, " . . . where the rule of law supplants the rule of the jungle. A world in which nations recognize the shared responsibility for freedom and justice. A world where the strong respect the rights of the weak . . .

"America and the world must support the rule of law. And we will."

As Shakespeare once said; Gimme a break. (Ducky Shakespeare, Detroit bookie, 1949). The United States, in good times and bad, has been about as committed to the rule of law as the Mafia.

We have invaded, intervened and incursed as it suited our purpose, and international law be damned. It is particularly embarrassing for Mr. Bush to lay pious claim to lawfulness when, as a member of the Reagan administration, he supported our brazen refusal to submit to the authority of the World Court when Nicaragua brought charges against us.

Nor did our invasions of Grenada and Panama do much to inspire universal respect for the rule of law. In every case we relied on our might to make us right. The only countries who believe in the rule of international law are weak countries, and precious little good it does them.

If Mr. Bush's foreign policy statements were egregious, his domestic remarks were pernicious. He said:

"Americans must never again enter any crisis, economic or military, with an excessive dependence on foreign oil and an excessive burden of federal debt."

Give him this: you've got to admire his gall. In office one-and-a-half years, eight years a vice-president, and he still talks about national problems as though he had no role in creating them. "Deficit? Foreign oil? Don't look at me; I was out of the loop. Still am."

Even so, I felt that Mr. Bush, having mentioned a couple of problems (which is more than his predecessor ever did), would then have to come up with ways of dealing with them. He might even utter the two words that are hemlock to his lips, *conservation* and *taxes*. I felt wrong.

His ideas for the conservation of energy never got beyond incentives for domestic oil and gas exploration, using alternative fuel sources and developing Alaskan energy sources "without damage to wildlife." ("And for my next trick, I'm going to turn this lump of coal into a robin.") George Bush is to energy conservation what Central Park muggers are to physical fitness.

And taxes? The closest he got to talking about them was his mention of "tax measures" to help cut the deficit: research incentives, IRAs for new homeowners, tax-deferred family savings accounts, incentives for enterprise zones and domestic oil drilling and lower taxes on capital gains.

Wait a minute! Isn't this where we came in? Isn't that a cut from the speech Ronald Reagan made in 1980, the one that got us in this mess in the first place?

George Bush wants to balance the federal budget by adding more tax breaks and loopholes to the tax code. That's like trying to bail out a leaky boat by passing out sieves to the crew.

It was a shameful performance. The least one might expect from a president as the nation, under threat of war, sinks deeper into a quagmire of debt is an attempt to deal with problems seriously and honestly. Instead Mr. Bush chose to make a campaign speech.

The president also said: "So if ever there was a time to put country before self and patriotism before party, that time is now."

That was the most cynical cut of all. (1990)

War Leader

There are times when George Bush's attempts to be like Ronald Reagan are so inept as to be endearing, in the manner of a small boy wearing his father's clothes. Tuesday's State of the Union speech was one of those times.

Oh, he got a tremendous ovation when he paid tribute to "the hard work of freedom" being performed by "every man and woman now serving in the Persian Gulf," but that was no great accomplishment. The audience was made up largely of the same dolts who voted to put our young men and women needlessly at risk in the Gulf. They'd *better* be enthusiastic about the enterprise.

But Bush couldn't even pull off the touching-letter-from-a-brave-citizen trick. Just about every time Ronald Reagan gave a speech he'd pull out a letter he just got from some nobody and read it, just as though he didn't have a teleprompter. It would be from a little Elsie Blodgett in Flyover, Missouri, and she'd want to know if there were a Santa Claus.

He'd assure her (and us) that there was and that he hated taxes and by the time he was done there wasn't a dry eye in the house, unless you counted Jim Wright's. It was hokey, but comforting.

Bush tries hard but he lacks the Reagan touch. He pulled out a letter but kept squinting at the teleprompter as he slid sideways into a quotation from a Kathy Blackwell of Cape Cod—"My heart is aching, and I think that you should know—your people out here are hurting badly." You couldn't figure out whether it was her heart aching or his and whether it was over the war or the recession. It was a botch.

My favorite part of the speech, though, was when he went to the gallery. That's another thing Reagan always did. He'd introduce some local hero from Terribly Far, Montana, to represent the little people of the nation.

So Bush points to the gallery and says: "We all have a special place in our hearts for the families of our men and women serving in the Gulf. They are represented here tonight by Mrs. Schwarzkopf."

Mrs. Schwarzkopf? You pay tribute to the little people with the wife of a general? What's the matter, was Mrs. Quayle busy?

He would have been better off reading a letter from Mrs. Schwarzkopf and pointing to Kathy Blackwell in the balcony.

Another thing: I think we should stop calling it a "volunteer" army. We have a volunteer army only in the sense that General Motors has a volunteer work force; no one forced the workers to take their jobs. But volunteer sounds as though our service people got together and said: "Little Kuwait is in trouble, gang. We'd better join up." The most you can say about most of the people in our armed forces is that they took a chance that nothing terrible would happen if they enlisted and they lost their bet.

Perhaps the most disappointing thing about Mr. Bush's speech was how little he asked of us as a nation. He talked sacrifice but when it came down to specifics all he demanded were more tax breaks.

I think that's a mistake. I go back to World War II when Franklin D. Roosevelt was able to engage the entire nation in the war effort through mechanisms like income surtaxes and rationing.

There was no great need for gasoline rationing during the war, you know. We had a lot of gas. What rationing did, however, was give everyone a sense of participation and contribution.

It was the same with paper drives. I remember getting time off from class to go out and collect bundles of newspapers. I can't imagine that all that paper was very valuable to the war effort, but it gave even me—a nine-year-old—a role in the war. We were also encouraged to buy war bonds at less than market interest rates.

World War II was the last time an American president asked the nation to make personal sacrifices for a war. It is not coincidental that it was the last popular war.

Had President Bush proposed something like a war tax, however, all those flag-waving jingoes in Congress, whose eyes well up with tears at the very mention of our brave boys and girls in the Persian Gulf, would have exploded in outrage. War is one thing; taxes are another.

I think the American people might feel a lot less hypocritical if their support of the troops required something beyond waving flags and getting mad at peace protesters. On the other hand, they might not. Our capacity for hypocrisy grows by the day.

Which may explain why even so maladroit a mountebank as Mr. Bush is 80 percent in the polls and climbing. (1991)

3

THERE IS A BOMB IN GILEAD

I'M OFTEN ACCUSED of being a cynic, but I must confess to being taken in by the peace scare of 1989. The Berlin Wall went down. Eastern Europe, like a caged bird, was released to the sky. There was glasnost; there was perestroika. The Cold War was over and, by God, we'd won. We were ready to study war no more and beat our pruning hooks into plowshares . . . or whatever. Was it really only two years ago?

Good News

The Cold War is over; we've won. There was no way we could lose, actually. The Soviet Union simply could not match our bigger, more powerful economy in the waste of productive resources. While we were made weak by the exercise, the Soviets were bled white.

It's not that Mikhail Gorbachev is a nice guy or that he wishes us well, he merely has the courage to face reality. And the reality is that the Soviet Union cannot prosper and compete in the world marketplace if it continues to squander its resources in a senseless arms race and in maintaining an empire that brings it no profit.

We are confronted by exactly the same reality had we but wit to see it—not as sharply drawn perhaps, but similar. Last week news broke that the Perkin-Elmer Corporation, unable to find an American buyer for its state-of-the-art superconductor equipment business, was contemplating its sale to a Japanese firm.

The sale would surrender the future of computer chip manufacturing to the Japanese and make this country totally dependent on Japan for technological innovation in the field.

And the reason no American company could buy Perkin-Elmer? Because no American firm felt it could afford the research and development costs demanded by the technology. The Japanese, whose government subsidizes such investments, could.

We're sitting here spending our research money on missiles which we bury in the ground to scare the Russians while the Japanese and Germans, free of such burdens, seize control of the technology of the twenty-first century.

Within the past week the Air Force announced that it was going ahead with its plans to put 50 MX missiles on railroad tracks to make them less vulnerable to surprise attack. And CIA Director William Webster said that the political change in eastern Europe will require a bigger CIA budget.

So maybe the good news isn't so good. Maybe we didn't win the Cold War after all; maybe the Japanese and Germans did.

I knew I could find a dark lining in the silver cloud if I looked hard enough. I feel better now. (1989)

How Green Was My H-Bomb

Congress has its faults—it is for the most part cowardly, venal and self-aggrandizing—but give it this: it is absolutely ingenious in its efforts to protect the military budget from the scourge of peace.

Senator Sam Nunn, Democrat-Georgia, reached new heights of creativity last week when he proposed giving our military responsibility for protecting the environment.

"I believe that America must lead the way in marshaling a global response to the problems of environmental degradation, and the defense establishment should play an important role in this effort," said Senator Nunn. To that end he proposed a "Strategic Environmental Research Program," which would enlist the resources and talent of the military and intelligence communities to address environmental threats.

The amazing part about it is that he was able to deliver the proposal with a straight face and that the nation's press reported it without a knowing smirk. His colleagues, of course, were giddy with delight.

"What's really great about this is that Sam is really into it," said Senator Timothy Wirth, Democrat-Colorado.

And Senator Albert Gore, Democrat-Tennessee, said: "Philosophically, it's a watershed."

It sure is. Up to now we have demanded at least some tenuous military justification for spending money on the military; protection against the armed legions of Nicaragua, a leak-proof umbrella to fend off Soviet missiles, something.

But with this new proposal we have moved into an open field where virtually no military expenditure need go unjustified. If the Defense Department could make a security threat out of Grenada, imagine what it will do with global warming.

It is tempting to dismiss the proposal as another wacko idea from Congress, silly on its face, and let it go at that. The job of the military, after all, is to destroy the environment, not save it. Putting the environment in the care of the military-industrial complex is like boarding your pet cat at an alligator farm.

But Sam Nunn is no wacko. He is one of the most persistent and effective congressional friends the Pentagon has. In suggesting that the military be enlisted in the war against environmental degradation, he is protecting not so much the environment as the military budget.

Since the virtual collapse of the Soviet threat, our military has been thrashing around for a new mission. It's either that or turn back some of the $300 billion it eats up every year. Terrorism, drugs, Castro . . . all have been auditioned for the role of Chief Threat and been found wanting.

This environmental scam is the latest attempt to fill the Menace Gap. The military has grasped it with the enthusiasm of a drunk reaching for a free drink. "Obviously, we like the direction," a Pentagon spokesperson said of the proposal.

As well they should. The Bush administration, along with Congress, has been unconscionable in its reluctance to make significant cuts in the military budget. Defense Secretary Richard Cheney's latest budget proposal suggests an after-inflation cut of 1 percent in military spending. This from a budget that is still heavy with fat from the wasteful military buildup of the Reagan years.

That can't go on indefinitely. Sooner or later the public will figure out that we're spending $300 billion to protect ourselves from an enemy that has lost interest in us. So Nunn has suggested dusting off a real threat—albeit one that the Bush administration has all but ignored so far—and putting the military to work on it.

Some will say that it smacks of the National Defense Highway Act, in which the Eisenhower administration used the excuse of national security to justify the construction of the interstate highway system. President Eisenhower had the wit, however, not to trust the actual building of the roads to the military.

Our military-industrial complex today is a gigantic, self-perpetuating machine in which money goes in one end and toys of dubious utility come out the other. This week it was revealed that the performance of our state-of-the-art Stealth fighter was less than scintillating when it was used in the invasion of Panama last year and that its failure to hit its bombing target had been covered up by the Air Force.

Hey, it flew, didn't it? What do you expect for $4 billion?

Throw away your fur caps and your mittens, you folks up there in Alaska. Put in a back-up air conditioner, Houston. If the Pentagon has been unleashed on global warming, it will soon be June in January. (1990)

Helping the Russians

You're probably not going to believe this, but last week there was a card-carrying Communist nosing around the White House, looking into corners, opening drawers, and nobody so much as notified the FBI. As a matter of fact, the White House staff was helping him.

The fellow was Mikhail Shkabardnya, a top Kremlin aid, and he was there to get tips on how to run a presidency. The Russians are new to this game, after all—the office of president of the Soviet Union was set up just this spring—so they sent this Shkabardnya here to find out how things work. John Sununu, White House chief of staff, has promised to visit Moscow this summer to give him on-site instruction.

I'd love to go with him and listen to what goes on. I'll bet it will be something like this:

"Welcome to our humble Kremlin, Mr. Chief of Staff. It is great honor having you here. Please excuse howling mob outside; is group of Lithuanians celebrating national liberation day."

"I didn't know Lithuanians had a national liberation day."

"They don't. That's what howling is about."

"I wouldn't worry about it if I were you. It's been my experience that the television networks get bored with any protest that goes on longer than two days. After that the demonstrators are just another bunch of kooks that you can ignore, like the homeless."

"Excellent, your Chiefship. Is exactly kind of tip we were hoping to get from you."

"Glad to be of service. What else did you want to know?"

"We are wondering, how does White House staff get information from the departments of government to president?"

"Pardon me?"

"Is big government, much information. Do you make long reports for president to read? Do cabinet ministers speak in conference? Is there digest? What?"

"I don't think we're on the same page here, Mikhail. As a chief of staff the last thing you want is for information to reach your president. If he gets information, he'll know what's going on. If he knows what's going on, people will hold him responsible for what happens. If people hold him responsible, he doesn't get re-elected, and you're out of a job. A president must be kept ignorant at all costs."

"You mean President Reagan *really* didn't know trade with Iran was arms-for-hostages? Was not just alibi?"

"If they'd have told him they'd have had to tell everybody. The last American president who knew what was going on was Jimmy Carter. I rest my case."

"But if president has no information, how does he make decisions?"

"That's the whole point, Mikhail. You don't want your president making decisions. Decisions are what get you in trouble. There has never been a decisive president who ranked high in the opinion polls."

"With no information and no decisions, how does president deal with national problems?"

"With speeches. We've learned that if you identify a problem and make a speech about it, people don't expect you to do anything about it."

"Is amazing, this democracy. I don't know why we are not trying it long ago. What is role of free press in your government?"

"Crucial. You can't have a free government without a free press. That's why it's important to keep it under control at all times."

"But how? You have press protected by First Amendment."

"For the time being, yes. But all you have to do to neutralize it is give the press corps enough press releases and photo opportunities to keep it busy and throw them an occasional press conference where you don't answer the questions. If you do that and call them by their first names you can do anything you want and they'll never find out."

"Is that in spirit of glasnost?"

"Back home they call it investigative reporting."

"But what to do about problem that won't go away or keep quiet. Problem like Boris Yeltsin, for example."

"Don't look on Yeltsin as a problem, look on him as an opportunity. He is to you what the Democratic Party is to us, the disloyal opposition you can blame everything on—shortages, ethnic riots, bad weather, everything. If you didn't have Yeltsin you'd have to invent him."

"I am beginning understand. No information, no decisions, no news, no responsibility for action, no action."

"That's the ticket. And if something comes up you can't handle, don't hesitate to give a call on the hot line. You'll never learn how to be a democracy if you don't ask questions."

"Actually, is not so different from what we had before. Only voluntary." (1990)

The China Card

I was on my way to do some Christmas shopping when the familiar cry of "Hey you, columnist!" stopped me in my tracks. I turned, knowing who it was; a rather disagreeable chap who accosts me on the street from time to time in hopes of alleviating his ignorance.

It being easier to answer his questions than get rid of him, I said: "What can I do for you?"

"There's something I want you to explain," he said.

"I thought there might me. What is it?"

"The world. For instance, why did we send those two Kissinger guys, Eaglesomething and Stow . . . Snow . . ."

"Lawrence Eagleburger and Brent Scowcroft."

"Yeah, them . . . to China to make nicey-nicey with the Chinese thugs who were responsible for the massacre of students at Tiananmen Square last summer. I thought we weren't going to have anything to do with those blood-stained butchers."

"And we didn't," I replied, "for six whole months."

"Six months! Leona Helmsly got a stiffer sentence."

"Yes, but she didn't have Henry Kissinger for a lawyer. You can't hold grudges forever. China is an important country, and we have to deal with it as it is. After all, the world didn't ostracize us when we killed those students at Kent State twenty years ago, did it? In international affairs they call it realpolitik."

"I thought maybe we could have at least asked them to apologize. You know, like, 'We're sorry; the troops went off accidentally.' Something like that."

"That would be rude."

"I guess so. That real politics thing is probably for the best in the long run. It means we can cut the military budget way back."

"Why do you say that?"

"Well, you know, we had this big military establishment because we were afraid that Russia was going to attack us or invade Europe. So it's not going to happen; Russia's standing out there with its pants around it's ankles. We can start doing something useful with the money we've been spending on defense."

"That kind of talk is what led to World War II. As Dan Quayle so aptly put it, nothing has changed and it could change back in a minute. We must never forget that the Russians are very liberal Marxist-Leninist Communists who are committed to world domination. You can't trust them."

"You mean we can trust the Chinese because they shot down their protesters, but not the Russians because they didn't?"

"Exactly."

"What about Central America then? If we can live with China, why can't we live with the Sandinistas in Nicaragua? They're not as Communist as the Chinese, and they kill retail, not wholesale."

"Because we have an obligation to the Contras, that brave band of freedom-fighters who are seeking to throw off the yoke of Marxist-Leninism and turn Nicaragua into Switzerland, only with bananas."

"Is that why they keep making raids into the countryside and killing villagers?"

"There's an election coming up and, admittedly, sometimes their voter registration drives get out of hand. Still, they're better than the alternative."

"Which is?"

"George Bush making the right wing mad."

"I suppose if we support the right of the Contras to overturn an oppressive government, we feel the same way about the rebels in El Salvador, right?"

"Wrong. There, Communist rebels are attempting to overthrow the freely elected government which we put in office. They must be stopped at all costs."

"Excuse me, but is that the freely elected government that killed those six priests and tore out their brains awhile ago?"

"The government didn't do that. It's just as puzzled by the incident as we are. There's some thought the priests might have committed suicide, just to make the government look bad."

"And tore out their own brains?"

"Precisely."

"Gee, that makes everything clear. Thanks, columnist. If it weren't for guys like you, guys like me would be confused about our foreign policy."

He went off then. I wish I'd had time to tell him the key to our foreign policy of the moment. Richard Nixon.

Just as Mr. Nixon's malignant spirit has invaded the soul of the Republican Party's electioneering mechanism, so has his foreign policy become that of the nation.

He invented George Bush, after all, just as he invented Henry Kissinger. By coincidence, Eagleburger and Scowcroft left the employ of Mr. Kissinger to take up government jobs just as Mr. K. was starting China Ventures, a firm dedicated to making investments in China. How surprising could it have been that Eagleburger and Scowcroft were Mr. Bush's chosen emissaries to rebuild bridges to China?

A couple of weeks ago I said that I'd feel better if Nixon were running our foreign policy. Forget I said it. He is.

Now I'd feel better if I was sure he was on our side. (1989)

Anschluss Junior

Suddenly the woods are full of experts on East Germany. Click on the television set and, more than likely, there's one of them yammering about how the collapse of the Berlin Wall is the greatest thing since Ovaltine or more dangerous than bad brakes or, in some cases, both.

Not only have the usual suspects—George Kennan, Paul Nitze, George Ball, Henry the K., Zbigniew Brzezinski, that crowd—weighed in with their opinions, but every jerkwater college in the country seems to have a resident eastern European expert willing to be interviewed on the subject. They have one thing in common.

They don't know what they're talking about.

They're like stock market experts. After the stock market does something sensational, the experts can tell you exactly why it happened. But ask them to predict what the market will do next and they give you the round eyes and the shrug.

That's what our foreign policy experts are doing right now. The events of the past few weeks in eastern Europe are breathtaking in their speed and scope. A flood made up of equal parts of freedom and consumer lust has swept through Poland, Bulgaria, Hungary, East Germany and through parts of the Soviet Union itself, leaving the Communist party behind it, clinging to the tops of poles.

The most radical event, of course, is the sudden opening of the borders between East and West Germany. It not only promises to change the map of Europe, but the mindset that has informed international relations for the past forty years.

I see it as a good news–bad news joke.

The good news is that another country has cast off the shackles of Communism and breathed the air of free men and women.

The bad news is that the country is East Germany.

Moved as I am at the touching sight of those East Germans streaming over the border to take a look at the candy store called West Berlin, there is a part of me that feels as though Charlie Manson just got a parole.

You think I'm being anti-German, don't you? Not a bit of it. Germans make great cars; I wouldn't leave home without one. They also do well with beer and tennis players. But I am also mindful of the fact that when crowds of Germans overrun a border they are generally wearing helmets. And if they're not they soon will be.

The terrible history of the twentieth century is largely the story of a Germany trying to gather the German-speaking peoples to its Teutonic breast. And should they get another language group or two mixed in there, accidents happen.

There is hardly a nation in the Western world that has not suffered grievously at the hands of Germans trying to reconstitute the fatherland. Is it any wonder then, that the current effort of the severed snake to pull itself together again is causing a sense of unease behind the euphoria at seeing the Communist empire crash?

The leaders of the world have been quick to assure us that reunification of Germany is not in the cards or, at the very least, far in the distance. Perhaps, but once the borders between East and West Germany have opened and once East Germany ceases to be a Communist state—as seems altogether likely now—East Germany becomes a political vacuum. And, as Isaac Newton once said: "Nature abhors a vacuum and that's all the excuse Germany needs." (Or he would have said it if he'd thought of it.)

President Bush thus far has reacted to what's happening in eastern Europe with his customary sense of urgency. He sits there in his canoe, letting his hand trail in the water. That's his answer to everything.

I don't pretend to know what's going to happen, but I wouldn't be surprised if somewhere deep in the bowels of the Pentagon, or perhaps the White House, there were a task force at work trying to think up another Global Menace.

The Communist Menace is just about played out. How evil can an empire be when it is everywhere in retreat of its borders? Castro is a pathetic, lonely figure, trapped in a time-warp. Ortega is a two-bit drugstore cowboy, Noriega not much more.

You can't keep the military-industrial complex humming along at $300 billion a year on threats like that. Not even the American people are that dumb.

Maybe a reunified, rearmed Germany, longing to reclaim its lost Polish lands, is the answer. (1989)

I needn't have worried about Germany. By a remarkable coincidence, just as we were preparing to dismantle the military-industrial complex, we fell into a just war against an evil dictator that renewed our faith in phantasmagoric weapons systems. Without these weapons—missiles so smart that you can show them a sock and they will find the owner and bomb him—we would have been a pitiful, helpless giant at the mercy of Arab despots and liberal Democrats.

I make no charges.

4

DAS KAPITAL, GERFLUNKEN

I DON'T OFTEN brag this around, but I, too, was infected with the lust of the 1980s. Yes, I, too, tried to get rich. There's something to be said for infiltrating the enemy and reforming from within, you know. I count it high among my liberal credentials that I failed miserably.

A Bernard Baruch, He's Not

I don't expect much out of life. I don't wish for world peace or an end to hunger or good television; nothing unattainable. I have but one simple desire.

I want to be filthy rich, and I don't want to work for the money.

Is that too much to ask, the same break that the du Ponts, Rockefellers and Kennedys get? Apparently so. I seem destined to live my life as one of the working poor.

The final realization came to me recently when the stock market crashed. I came into some money last year and sank it into the stock market. "What have I got to lose?" I asked myself. "I didn't really do anything to earn the money, anyway."

A voice inside me answered, "Just because you didn't earn it doesn't mean it's not money."

I ignored it. If you want to be a Rockefeller and you've chosen Kowalskis for parents, you have to take risks. I took every nickel and bought stocks.

And the results were terrific. The stock market kept going up and my stocks with it. September, October, November; nothing but blue skies. December was even better. Every day was a wedding.

Then my mother came to stay with us over the holidays; a very nice, Polish lady from Florida, by way of Detroit.

Every morning, while I was chortling over my unrealized capital gains, she'd say:

"You should get out of the stock market, son. The stock market is not for people like you."

"What do you mean, people like me? What am I, one of the Three Stooges?"

"No, you're not, but you're not T-bone Pickens either."

"Mom, I'm making money. Leave me alone."

It became a daily ritual. I'd tell her how much money I made the day before and she'd say: "Sell."

Her visit at its end, I took her to the airport. "It was wonderful seeing you, dear," I told her. "Sell," she answered.

The following Thursday the market went down eighty-six points, and I lost more money than I'd made in my first year of gainful employment. That's not as much as it sounds (I was a newspaper reporter), but to me it was a breathtaking amount still.

My mother called: "So you didn't listen to me, did you, Big Shot? When I told you to sell, you thought: What does this foolish old woman know? She's Polish. Well, I know what your father always used to say; I know that much."

"They're all in it together."

"Darn right. Look how the market acts. One day it goes way down, the next day nothing changes and it goes way up. You think that's an accident?"

"Admittedly, the market has been volatile lately, but that's because the big brokerages and funds have these computerized buy and sell programs now that are triggered automatically."

"What do you mean, automatically? You think those people on Wall Street sit there and lose money automatically? These arbitrashers, I heard about them on C-Span, they make money when the market goes up and they make money when it goes down. And when it goes up and down like a yo-yo, they make more. If they didn't, they'd tell their machines to do something else automatically. Use your head, Sonny; that's why we sent you to college. The whole thing is fixed. The little guy doesn't have a chance."

"You're going to have to take my word on this, Mom; I know what I'm doing. My advisers say this is just a blip in a long-term bull market."

"Good for them. I say what they're telling you is a lot of bull; but don't listen to me, I'm only your mother."

"It's going to be all right. I'm still ahead of the game."

"OK, but don't say I didn't warn you. I have to go now; tonight's my pinochle night."

"Have a good time, Mom."

"So long, sucker."

The next day the market suffered its worst loss—ever.

That night, the phone rang. I knew who it was.

"What did I tell you?" she began. "The worst loss in history, worse than 1929 even. I warned you."

"Yeah, but the market is bigger now. In percentage terms . . ."

"Percentage, perschmentage, all I know is that the crash is here. Get out before it's too late."

"This is a temporary loss; nothing to get excited about, Mom. It's a technical correction brought about by profit-taking."

"Sure, that's what they said in 1929."

"Mom, I'm not a speculator, I'm an investor. I'm in good, solid stocks. I know what I'm doing. Trust me."

"I guess I was wrong."

"You mean you admit it?"

"Sure. You are one of the Three Stooges," she said. And she hung up.

The phone rang again in three minutes. It was her. "Sell," she said, and hung up again.

My mind turned to a story told about Joe Kennedy, the patriarch of the Kennedy family. It may be apocryphal, but that's OK. Apocryphal stories are always the most instructive.

It is said that while having his shoes shined one day in August of 1929, Kennedy overheard the shoeshine men at the stand talking about their investments in the stock market. They talked about the stocks they owned, the stocks they might buy and the money they were making.

Mr. Kennedy walked off of that shoe shine stand, went straight to the office of his broker and sold all of his stocks. If the stock market boom was being fueled by the enthusiasm of people who shined shoes for a living, he reasoned, maybe it wasn't as good as it looked. Three months later, the market crashed, leaving the Kennedy fortune intact.

It occurs to me that I'm a little like those shoeshine men. If the market is attracting people like me, maybe it's time to sell.

I finally did sell, just as the market bottomed out. It's been going up ever since.

I am reconciled to the fact that the only way I'm ever going to be filthy rich is if a du Pont or a Rockefeller adopts me and I don't expect that to happen. Fifty-five-year-olds are notoriously hard to place. (1987)

But for the most part I was to mine own self, true. Throughout the 1980s I kept telling them that the sky was about to fall, that the wolf was at the gates of the city. They laughed at me. I became the object of scorn and ridicule in certain circles. I was not helped by the fact that every time I yelled "Wolf!" a St. Bernard would appear. No matter; the St. Bernard keeps getting meaner.

I take no pleasure in announcing the obvious, that the nation's economy is on the skids. I, too, would prefer to be as cheerful as a fortune cookie. Professional responsibility, however, dictates otherwise.

So it didn't happen in the 1980s, but it's going to happen in the 1990s. The sky is going to fall. The wolf is about to enter the city.

And when it happens, I'm going to love saying, "I hate to say I told you so, but . . ."

Early Warning Signal (1985)

Hark! What was that sound? Was it the distant crack of our ice floe beginning to break up? Was it the muffled roar of an approaching avalanche on the mountain above us? Hard to tell.

This much is sure: The banking crisis in Ohio that followed the collapse of a Cincinnati savings and loan made a sound that reverberates throughout our financial system. An *ominous* sound.

Don't worry about it, they tell us. The Ohio situation is unique. The affected Ohio savings and loans aren't insured by the federal government, but by a private firm. When the Cincinnati savings and loan took a bath on its dealings with a Florida investment firm, it went belly-up, and its losses are expected to drain all available funds in the state's insurance pool. Naturally, the investors in savings and loans that depend on that same pool made a run for it, and the state declared a bank holiday to decide what needed to be done.

Yes, that's a special situation, but basically, all situations are special. If you had gone to an Ohio savings and loan official a month ago and asked him how things were, be assured that he'd have said: "Terrific. Never better. Nothing to worry about." The fact remains that the collapse of a single sleazy Florida investment company has triggered a chain of events that has produced financial chaos in one of our largest states.

Do you really think that Florida firm is the only one with that kind of potential for mischief? Don't be silly. It made its living buying and selling federal bonds, supposedly the safest of investments. If it can go under and take an entire state savings and loan system with it, there have to be other time bombs ticking in our financial system.

Consider the fact that President Reagan's first term in office saw the national debt nearly double and that, if Congress gives him *all* the cuts in domestic spending that he asked for in his budget, the national debt will increase by more than $180 billion next year.

Consider the fact that in the next few months we will become a debtor nation for the first time since 1919 and that by the end of the year we will probably pass Brazil as the most indebted country on earth.

Consider the fact that the other great debtor countries—Brazil, Mexico and Argentina—have hardly a hope of paying off what they owe. They need restructuring of their loans simply to keep up with the interest. The reason they can get such restructuring is that the alternative—the bankruptcy of one or more of them—is likely to cause a collapse of the international banking system.

Consider the fact that Iowa banks, to pick out one state among many, are carrying a high percentage of loans that are no longer fully covered by collateral because the value of the land offered as collateral has fallen below the value of the outstanding loan. As banks foreclose on these loans and sell off the land, the price of land drops still further and more loans come into jeopardy.

Consider the fact that none of these problems—not one—is being seriously addressed by our elected representatives. The president tells us that everything is peachy and is going to get peachier; all we have to do is build more missiles. The Democrats say that we have to be nicer to poor people and everything will be all right.

That doesn't make sense to me, none of it. You don't have to be a financial genius to sense that there is something very wrong out there, that there are powerful forces gathering against our continued well-being and that we're not preparing to meet them.

When one looks back to periods that preceded the great disasters of history, one is almost always appalled by the blindness and stupidity of the people of the time. Take World War I. Viewed at this distance it seems utterly incomprehensible that the most civilized nations on earth could stumble into so savage and avoidable a conflict. Same with the Depression. Why couldn't intelligent people see that coming? All the signs were there.

I wonder what future historians will say of the present era. That the crack of the ice was mistaken for the creaking of the house in the wind? That the roar of the avalanche was drowned out by the hiss of the television set? We'll see.

Apropos of the failed savings and loan in Cincinnati: a friend once heard Elliot Janeway, the acerbic financial consultant, speak to a group of savings and loan executives in Cincinnati.

"Every town has its famous heroes," he told them. "London has Jack the Ripper, Chicago has Al Capone. And Cincinnati has its savings and loan associations."

They don't call him "Calamity Janeway" for nothing. I fear his time of wisdom is fast approaching. (1985)

Foreign Debt

I had a friend in high school named Ernie who was a whiz with money. He had some, for one thing, and he was willing to lend it, for another. Whenever you were absolutely desperate for cash you could go to Ernie and hit him up.

The thing is, if you borrowed, say, five dollars, Ernie would take back a dollar of it immediately and still expect you to pay back the full five when the loan came due in a week or two. Interest. And if you were still short when your time was up, Ernie would call Sonny over.

Sonny was huge, the third-string tackle on the football team. He'd have been the starter except that he couldn't go more than three plays without being called for unnecessary roughness. I don't think he understood the penalty; he didn't think there was such a thing as unnecessary roughness.

With Sonny at his side, Ernie would say something like:

"I'll give you one more week, but it's gonna cost you more interest. And if you don't pay next week, I'm going to let Sonny break your legs, which he's been wanting to do."

I don't recall Sonny ever breaking anyone's legs, but I don't recall anyone not paying up either. They were a great team.

I sometimes wonder what Ernie is doing now. My guess is that he's either in jail or he's an international banker, maybe both.

The technique is the same. The banks make loans, some of them bad loans to bad risks. Then when the hapless debtor is unable to pay, the bankers bring in their powerful governments to enforce the terms by breaking legs.

A couple of weeks ago I was in Brazil, sitting on an idyllic oceanside terrace, talking about Brazil's economic problems with my friends Carlos and Monique, who are Argentine. Brazil had just suspended interest payments on its international debt. I said that it was almost incomprehensible to me that a country like Brazil, rich in both natural and human resources, should be in such straits.

Monique slammed down her glass.

"We are all colonies," she said. "We need hospitals and roads and schools and instead we work to pay your banks."

"But you did borrow the money, didn't you?" I asked.

"No," she said. "The money was given to the generals who ran the countries. They spent some on self-protection and put the rest in Swiss bank accounts. If your banks want their money, they should go to Switzerland."

"Come on," I said. "What about the economic development money?"

Carlos, Monique's husband, smiled. "We have a joke in Argentina," he said. "In the old days an Argentine general went to Brazil and was invited to dinner at a Brazilian general's home. He was amazed to find that his Brazilian counterpart lived in a palace, a huge mansion with fountains and battalions of servants. After dinner he pulled his host aside and said, 'Please don't think me forward, but how can you afford all of this on a military man's salary?'

"The Brazilian led his guest to the window and pointed at a large suspension bridge in the distance. 'Do you see that bridge?' he said.

" 'Yes,' said the Argentine.

" 'I built that bridge and there was enough left over for all of this.'

"Two years pass and the Brazilian general has occasion to visit Argentina. He pays a call on his friend and is amazed to find that the Argentine general's home is even larger than his own, with more fountains and the servants more lavishly dressed.

" 'But how did you manage it?' he asks.

"The Argentine strides to the window and points to an empty landscape. 'Do you see that bridge?' he asks.

" 'No,' the Brazilian general says.

" 'I didn't build that bridge, and there was enough left over for all of this,' says the Argentine."

Carlos leaned back in his chair. "I suppose that in Brazil, they tell the story the other way around."

It raises a good point. When you loan money to vicious tyrants who abuse their people and steal from them, you should not expect to get back 100 cents on the dollar when the rascals are thrown out.

But banks do. Not because they're bad guys, not because they're good guys. Because they're banks.

It would seem to me that a country like ours, which is willing to spend hundreds of millions of dollars in military spending in hopes of keeping Communism out of this hemisphere, would be willing to spend a few bucks on helping the new democracies of Latin America out of the bog they're in. It's cheaper in the long run.

Oh well, we have this consolation:

When the rickety debt structure of the Latin countries comes crashing down, bringing our major banks with it, sending our stock market into a dive and triggering a depression, we'll be getting exactly what we deserve. (1987)

Who's Pearl Harbor?

Did I complain when the Japanese performed euthanasia on our television manufacturing industry? No. Did I say anything when they pushed aside our auto industry and seized world leadership? No. At least they gave us good televisions and cars.

Nor did I get upset when they bought Columbia Pictures. What's the worst that could happen? They change the company's name to "Corrumbia" and, in his next movie, Sylvester Stallone bombs Pearl Harbor. Big deal. I didn't even mind when they rented Ronald Reagan for a week; it's their money.

Now, however, they have gone too far. They've bought Rockefeller Center.

The deal is complex. Mitsubishi Estate Company bought 51 percent of the holding company that owns Rockefeller Center but Mitsubishi's share could slip to 20 percent in the future, depending on events. Still . . .

Rockefeller Center is more than just a pile of concrete and glass in the middle of Manhattan. It's more than the home of NBC and a host of classy shops across the street from St. Patrick's Cathedral.

It is, for some of us, nothing less than the ultimate symbol of urban sophistication. Young midwestern hicks like myself used to dream of going ice skating on the rink right there in the midst of those towering skyscrapers. We used to think about going up to the Rainbow Room at dusk and ordering up a dry martini as we watched the lights of the buildings flanking Central Park wink on. You could actually imagine Melvyn Douglas sitting at the next table, talking on a white telephone.

When I first started going to New York thirty-five years ago, there were two places above all others that announced that you were in the Big Apple. One was Times Square, at night. The other was Rockefeller Center, any time. They pulled down Times Square, and now they've sold Rockefeller Center to the Japanese.

Is nothing sacred? What will the Japanese buy next, Monticello? The Washington Monument? Johnny Carson?

I wouldn't be surprised. The sad truth is that in our acquisitive, market-oriented society, pretty much everything is for sale. Even as Japan is renting our former president, an airline collects a former speaker of the U.S. House of Representatives and a former secretary of state. A coffee company buys an ex-anchor person famed for her contempt of the establishment and baseball heroes sell their autographs. Doesn't anyone know how to be a hero anymore?

Some observers were puzzled when dozens of House Democrats defected from their leadership to support a capital gains tax cut that favored rich people. Weren't Democrats supposed to be the party of the poor and the working stiff?

Only if you count voters. If you look at *contributors* to political campaigns, it's a different ball game. As Representative Dan Glickman, a Kansas Democrat, told the *Washington Post* recently:

"It's as simple as he who pays the piper plays the tune. Money has made it more difficult for Democrats to define an economic agenda that is different from the Republican agenda; we are talking from the same contributors."

We have a rather more naked example of that same corruption of the spirit before us at the moment.

Five United States senators—one a legitimate war hero, one a former astronaut, one an ex-foreign correspondent, for goodness sakes—stand accused of interfering in the investigation of a failing savings and loan run by a big political contributor.

Common Cause, the goo-goo lobby, has asked the Senate Ethics Committee to look into the activities of Senators Alan Cranston (Democrat-California), Dennis DeConcini (Democrat-Arizona), John McCain (Republican-Arizona), John Glenn (Democrat-Ohio) and Don Reigle (Democrat-Michigan) on behalf of their supporter Charles Keating, the former head of Lincoln Savings and Loan, which collapsed a while ago leaving debts of $2.3 billion, payable by the U.S. taxpayer.

I know that a man is supposed to be considered innocent until proved guilty, but in the case of politicians we can make an exception. Politicians are always guilty of something: in this case, of taking a total of about $1.3 million in campaign contributions from Keating, then trying to intimidate Federal Home Loan Bank Board examiners who were trying to seize Keating's failing savings and loan.

One doesn't know whether the intimidation succeeded, but it took two years for the examiners to seize the savings and loan and close it, a delay that cost taxpayers some $1.3 billion in additional losses.

And these five are among the *better* people in the Senate. God only knows what the real crooks are costing us.

You see something you like? Anything at all? Make me an offer. I'm the United States of America. That saying about money not buying happiness is only true if owning a politician doesn't make you happy. (1989)

Glowing Crop Report

American industry does not get the credit it deserves. It gets held up to constant ridicule by critics who compare it to its Japanese or German counterparts. Admittedly, we have a problem or two. We can't make cars that work. We can't make steel that anyone wants to buy. Our television sets are on the endangered species list. Nobody's perfect.

But when it comes to sheer creativity, the ability to come up with ingenious solutions to seemingly insoluble problems, there's no one who can match us; the latest example of which was provided just the other day.

The *New York Times* reported that the Kerr-McGee Corporation was spraying thousands of acres of pastureland in eastern Oklahoma with a fertilizer made from radioactive wastes. They take the waste out of their nuclear plants, "neutralize" it, then put it out on the fields.

Talk about being handed a lemon and making lemonade with it!

One of the main problems at a nuclear plant is what to do with the waste material. Nobody wants it. It's expensive to get rid of, and it's dangerous. So what does Kerr-McGee do? They feed it to people.

Is this a great country, or what?

Eighteen million gallons of the stuff were sprayed on land bordering both sides of the Arkansas River this year, and the firm hopes to get a permit from the Nuclear Regulatory Commission to market the fertilizer commercially.

Does it make things grow? Are you kidding me? They've already found a frog with nine legs in one of the ponds that drains a treated pasture. Really.

There have also been unexplained deaths of farm animals and gross malformations of newborn livestock in the area.

Not to worry. "Bad things happen all the time," a company spokesperson told the *Times*. "Cattle die. Horses die. There are deformities of people wherever you go. Anything that happens in the area is automatically attributed to the fertilizer program."

Still, despite reassurances like that, people worry. You see, in addition to being radioactive, the fertilizer contains some toxic solvents and at least eighteen potentially poisonous heavy metals, including arsenic, lead, mercury, molybdenum, nickel, cobalt and cadmium. In heavy concentrations, such material can cause mutation, paralysis or death.

"When they spray, the smell knocks you over," one rancher said. "It burns your eyes and your throat. It's a terrible thing that's happening out there."

"Hysteria," the Kerr-McGee people retort. The radioactivity and heavy metal levels in their product are below those found in many commercial phosphate fertilizers, they say.

But that's not the point, is it? The point is the leap of imagination that took Kerr-McGee from nuclear waste to fertilizer.

I can just see the Kerr-McGee executives sitting around a conference table, brainstorming the waste disposal problem, when one of them lights up and says:

"How about making soap out of it? We could advertise it as the soap that glows in the dark."

"So we corner the market on people who take baths with the lights out. Forget it."

"I've got it! Why don't we freeze it and make popsicles out of it?"

"We tried that," another says. "It tasted funny and it turned the test kids' teeth black."

"So why don't we make fertilizer out of it? Who cares what fertilizer tastes like?"

Thus does genius manifest itself in these modern times. It reminds me of the solution Milo Minderbinder of *Catch-22* came up with when he got stuck with an entire crop of Egyptian cotton that he couldn't get rid of. He made it into cotton balls, coated them with chocolate and sold them as candy. Kerr-McGee's idea is better, though. Chocolate can be harmful to your health.

It's not as though the company didn't get proper permission to use the fertilizer, after all. True, it didn't get authorization from the Food and Drug Administration or the Environmental Protection Agency or the United States Department of Agriculture, but it didn't need to, it says. It got its permission from the Nuclear Regulatory Commission, which made its determination on the basis of studies provided by the corporation.

Kerr-McGee, by the way, is the company that operated the nuclear plant at which Karen Silkwood was protesting unsafe conditions when she met her still-mysterious death in a car accident in 1974. Some say she was deliberately run off the road late one night. I don't know why I mention that, it just occurred to me right here for some reason or other.

The main point to be made is that Kerr-McGee is an American company, giving us better living through chemistry. We ought to be proud. Isn't it wonderful to have an administration that keeps government off of our backs—and in our food chain? (1987)

A Modest Proposal

Take Texas . . . please.

I mean it. I've been studying the situation and I've come to the conclusion that the best way to balance the budget, lower taxes and raise the level of taste in this country by five basis points is to throw Texas out of the Union. For too long have we allowed ourselves to be victimized by that whining pack of fast-buck artists who, without irony, call themselves "The Lone Star State."

Texans talk a big game on the subject of self-reliance—they scorn giving help to welfare mothers and the homeless—but as soon as a cloud passes over their economic sun they are quick to form a line at the federal trough, begging for a handout. And they get it.

Consider the ongoing Great Savings and Loan Bailout and Barbeque. It really should be called the Texas bailout. Throughout the early 1980s Texas allowed swindlers and seat-of-the-pants promoters virtual free rein in the looting of their savings institutions. It wasn't a surreptitious operation; they gloried in it. Those bums bought themselves fleets of Rolls Royces, private airplanes and palatial vacation getaways as they financed projects that the Tooth Fairy would have found unrealistic. Texans thought they were cute.

When it all came crashing down the hustlers skipped town with the cash, and the depositors, most of them Texans, came sniveling to the federal government to make sure they didn't have to pay for having sought out unrealistically high interest rates with their savings. Is the government paying up? Is Kim Bassinger a girl?

No one knows what the savings and loan mess is going to cost; right now the low ball estimate is $200 billion. Almost half of that total will go to Texas. At current rates the bailout is going to provide Texas with a net inflow equal to $4,775 for every man, woman and child in the state. And it's only going to cost the rest of us taxpayers $1,387 apiece. They let us off easy this time.

The added irony of the situation is that should the economy manage to struggle out from its Texas burden to recover and start growing again, Texas is the place with all of those empty office buildings, shopping malls and housing developments—built with our money—waiting to accept the growth.

Lyndon Johnson was the quintessential Texas politician: a poor boy who came to Washington to make his fortune and did—in a federally regulated industry. In gratitude for granting him the chance to raid the treasury, he brought federal projects without number into his state and with them, federal money.

Jim Wright, another poor son of Texas, who rose to the speakership of the U.S. House of Representatives, started out selling books door to door. Unfortunately, that's the way he finished too. In between, his chief contribution to political science was his work in keeping regulators off the backs of savings and loan crooks and supporters until they could pick the vaults clean. I won't even mention John Connally.

When oil prices are high, Texas booms and lords it over the rest of us; when war threatens foreign oil supplies, Texas gouges. (Remember the Texas bumper sticker during the 1970s oil crisis: "Let the Bastards Freeze to Death in the Dark.") And whether prices are low or high, they come to Washington to whimper that they're being taxed to death.

What do we need with these people, anyway?

It's not as though it's a great cultural fount into which the rest of the country dips. Its chief cultural export—outside of chili that destroys the lining of the stomach—consists of hambone politicians who wear cowboy boots and funny hats.

The real question is not whether we should get rid of Texas, but how? You can't just let it loose on the world; the United Nations wouldn't stand for it.

I favor surrendering to Mexico.

I think we should run up a white flag over the Alamo and say: "O.K. Santa Anna, you win. We thought we could hold out, but you finally outwaited us. Come and get it, amigo."

There are very few nations that can resist accepting spoils of war, even when they're very spoiled.

It's a dirty trick to play on a nice country like Mexico, particularly when it has so many problems of its own, but we didn't get where we are by playing Mr. Nice Guy to Hispanics. We are struggling for economic survival and Texas hangs on our necks like a lead life preserver.

Mexico thinks it has problems now. Wait until it wakes up in bed with Texas. (1990)

Profile in Courage

Once upon a time there was a practically perfect congressman. He was loyal and brave and smart and caring and tough and able to brush after every meal. He was liberal where it was good to be liberal and conservative where it was good to be conservative and in all other things he was a flaming moderate. His greatest virtue, however, was his total honesty.

One day this congressman became frightened by the size of the federal budget. "A $200 billion deficit run year after year will destroy the economy," he said. "Something has to be done." He got a lot of favorable mail, along with editorials supporting his position, so he decided to give a speech to amplify his views. He hired a hall, and public television provided live coverage. He began:

"I'm not going to stand here and insult your intelligence by saying that we can cut the federal budget $200 billion a year just by doing away with waste and inefficiency. There isn't enough waste and inefficiency to go around. Nor am I going to tell you that we can solve the problem by cutting just nonmilitary spending or just military spending. And I'm not ready to raise taxes $200 billion. [Applause and hoots of appreciation.]

"I think we're all going to have to bear the burden of balancing the budget. Nonessential spending, both for military and social programs, will have to be cut, and tax loopholes will have to be closed. [More applause; shouts of "Close the loopholes!"]

"Now, to cut spending, I think you have to use the Willy Sutton theory of finance. You remember Sutton, the bank robber? When they asked Willy why he robbed banks, he said: 'Because that's where the money is.' [General laughter.]

"Well, you have to go where the money is to cut spending too. That's why I'm proposing a freeze on cost-of-living adjustments to Social Security and federal pensions, both civilian and military. [A stunned hush descends. An elderly man swinging a cane has to be restrained from attacking the speaker.]

"And I think we have to bring Medicare and Medicaid costs under control. To that end, I favor a cap being placed on doctors' fees and hospital charges. [A man in a plaid jacket, wearing a beeper, gets up and stalks out of the room, vowing to place the congressman's picture in hospital emergency rooms throughout the district.]

"Like most of you, I think military spending should be cut. But you can't do that simply by cutting a few exotic weapons systems. Most of our defense budget is taken up by personnel costs. To cut those costs, I propose reinstituting the draft and lowering military salaries. Young men and women should not have to be bribed into serving their country. To make sure that the draft is fair, I would do away with the deferment of college students. Conscientious objectors would be made to perform alternate service. [A Wagnerian woman at the back of the hall shouts, "Fascist swine!" Young people begin leaving.]

"As for tax loopholes, the one that will yield the most money is getting rid of the mortgage-interest deduction on your income tax. There's no reason to give homeowners a tax break that renters don't have. [The doors of the hall are clogged with people leaving. No one has been able to call into the television station for ten minutes.]

"I think we should tax health insurance benefits and unemployment benefits and treat capital gains just like any other income. [Racist! communist! elitist! shout members of the departing crowd.]

"And I also think we should have financial institutions withhold taxes from interest and dividend . . . [His voice trails off as he realizes that his audience has dwindled to a single person, and the television cameras have been shut off. He addresses that person.]

"Well, sir, I thank you for staying. Are you here as an individual citizen or do you represent a group?"

"A group," the man says. "I'm the executive director of the League of Left-Handed, Albino Hockey Players."

"I see. And can I count on your support in the coming election?"

"No. As a matter of fact, I'm your opponent in the coming election. That's the only reason I stayed."

Voters will forgive politicians many faults, but total honesty isn't one of them. (1983)

5

FATHERS AND SONS— AND DAUGHTERS

NOT ALL LIFE'S battles are fought against the invisible They, of course. Some of the most interesting conflicts are with people you love, especially your children. The interesting thing about them is that it sometimes takes twenty years to know whether you've won or lost.

I have three children, all grown. Well, at least they're tall. There are two great lessons they have taught me. One is that being a child doesn't teach you much about being a father.

The other lesson is that being a father doesn't teach you much about being a father, either.

Stop, He Explained

My father died nearly ten years ago, but I think of him often; never with more sympathy and understanding than when I recall the time he taught me to drive.

I suppose the tradition of teaching one's children how to drive has decayed with the advent of drivers' education classes, but in my day it was the solemn obligation of a father to instruct his children in the art of driving an auto. It was the children's obligation to endure it. That is the tradition we follow in my family, even today.

I was sixteen when I got my learner's permit and presented it to my father—not without some apprehension. He was a fine man, but limitless patience was not among his virtues. He did not suffer fools gladly, let alone teenage boys. He studied the permit and nodded his head slowly, as if in resignation.

"We'll go over to the Rouge Pools parking lot early Sunday morning," he said. "There shouldn't be anybody around then."

Nor was there when we got to the huge parking lot that Sunday and I got behind the wheel of our aging 1941 Pontiac. First came the lecture on the workings of the internal combustion engine (my father was a tool and die maker), then instructions on how to put the key in the ignition. Unbelievably, within an hour and a half I was actually driving; that is to say, I could start the car, put it in gear and let out the clutch slowly enough so that I achieved forward motion without stalling out. I was driving, I was steering; I felt triumphant.

Then we started to practice braking. My father said:

"You drive along and when I say 'Stop,' you stop."

"Yessir," I replied, and I drove along.

"Stop," my father said, and I came to a gentle, gliding halt, proud of myself.

"That wasn't fast enough," he said. "Do it again."

I did it again, and again, and again. Never fast enough. My foot would not do the bidding of my brain. Each time he said stop, I would coast to a stop. My father, his thin reserve of tolerance gone, moved to the edge of his seat and shook his finger in my face.

"Look," he said. "When I say stop, I want you to stop, dammit. Is that clear?"

"Yessir," I said.

"Then do it!"

I started up again, my sweating hands white on the steering wheel. I got up a pretty good head of steam.

"Stop!" my father yelled, as though he'd just spotted an infant in my path.

I nailed it. I jumped on that brake pedal and pushed down with everything I had. The wheels locked and the car went into a skid. My father was thrown from his perch into the windshield, striking his head with the sound of a watermelon being hit by a baseball bat. The sight of my father bouncing off the windshield so startled me that I took my foot off the brake, at which point the car lurched forward again, sending my father hurtling back to his seat. Panicked now, I slammed on the brakes again, and again my father flew forward head-first into the windshield with a thunk.

The car stopped this time, stalled out. My father sat there looking slightly ridiculous, with his hat battered and askew. I fought back a wild, suicidal impulse to laugh. We sat there for perhaps twenty seconds, in perfect silence.

Finally I said, "I don't think I want to have any more lessons today, Dad."

He nodded. "Yes, I think that's enough for today."

I eventually learned to drive, but just how is a blur. I recently asked my son if he remembered my teaching him how to drive.

"Oh yes," he said. "I'll never forget it."

"What was it like?"

"A nightmare. I couldn't get the hang of letting the clutch out, for some reason. We drove around for two hours with me stalling out the car and you getting quieter and quieter, pressing the words out between your lips. It was one of the worst experiences of my life."

A friend of mine happened by one day and taught him how to shift gears in fifteen minutes. I tried to teach my oldest daughter how to drive but it never worked out. She's twenty-seven now and neither drives nor wants to.

At present, I'm giving lessons to my youngest daughter. The other day I was teaching her how to brake, and I heard myself saying:

"You're stopping too slowly. When I say stop, I want you to stop, dammit. Is that clear?"

Thank God for seat belts.

It is not an easy job, being a father. I wish mine were here today so I could tell him how much I appreciated his efforts. He taught me all I know about raising children. (1986)

Ivy League Shopping

I spent part of my recent vacation shopping for a college for my daughter. She helped, of course; we went shopping together. It's still a year before her graduation from high school, but you can't start these things too soon, they tell me.

We got in the car and drove off into deepest Ohio. We'd stop at one school, take a tour, see an admissions officer, then hop back into the car and drive to another school. It was educational.

Do you know that there are schools out there that not only charge you twelve grand a year to get in, they expect you to be smart, too? That seems unfair, somehow. For twelve thou you should be able to go where you want. What's the sense of having rich parents if they can't buy you into places where you don't belong?

Not that my daughter is a dummy, understand; she's a smart kid. But she didn't have the foresight to be born to rich parents. My finances fall into an awkward category. I don't make enough money to send my children to the best schools, but I make too much to qualify for financial aid.

Oh, I could afford $12,000 a year if I had to, I suppose. It would involve a second mortgage and a night job driving a cab, but I could do it. The thing is, I'm not certain a college education is worth nearly $50,000. At least not for my daughter.

After a visit to one of the $12,000 schools, I asked my daughter how she liked the place.

"It was nice," she said, "but I'm not sure I'd have a very full social life if I went there."

A full social life! She expects me to lay out fifty big ones so that she can have a full social life! I told her that if she wanted a full social life, she should get a job in a bowling alley. For fifty grand I don't want her to have any social life at all. I don't want her looking up from her books.

I was the first member of my family to go to college; that includes my parents, grandparents, aunts, uncles, cousins—the first one. My father and I did not go shopping for a college. College was college; you either went or you didn't. If you went, you got to work in a white shirt and tie for the rest of your life; if you didn't, you faced a future of heavy lifting.

My father paid my tuition, which was $80 a semester. I can only imagine his face if I had come home and told him that I didn't want to go to that school because I was afraid I wouldn't have a full social life. It was bad enough when I told him I was becoming an English major.

For him, work lacked a certain meaning unless you did it with your hands. He had wanted me to become a dentist, and we had finally compromised by my becoming an engineering major. I was a miserable failure as an engineering student, and when I told him I was switching to English there was a long pause while he digested the information. Finally, he said:

"You're going to be a teacher? You're going to teach English?"

"No, Dad," I told him. "I'm going to be a writer." He was thunderstruck. Being a writer was something people in the movies did. Real life was harder. You had to be practical.

He took out extra life insurance shortly after that. He felt that it was going to have to provide for both my mother and me. Nor did he ever really change his mind, even when I became a modest success. He'd read one of my columns and say:

"Don't you think you ought to get a sideline? Something to fall back on in case they ever get wise to you?"

I wonder what he'd say if he knew that his son was shopping for a $50,000 education for his granddaughter. He probably would have recalled the time I fell off the front porch when I was ten years old and hit my head. To tell you the truth, he was never sure that eighty bucks a semester was such a hot investment.

Times change. (1983)

Money for Marrying

We married off our eldest daughter Leslie last week. It was a beautiful ceremony; the bride, if I do say so myself, was stunning, and the groom, David, was astonishly dapper. It was the first time I'd seen him in a suit. He is a painter; of paintings, alas, not houses.

I am not a sentimental man, but I am frank to admit I was close to tears during most of the proceedings. I kept thinking of how much they were costing me. Usually when I spend that kind of money I get something with windshield wipers.

I was not for a fancy wedding. Early on I had suggested that the couple elope. "What say I give you two lovebirds a couple of grand and you run off somewhere," I said to my daughter. "I know a good justice of the peace."

That kind of suggestion can get you killed when you make it in the presence of a bride, her mother and grandmother. All three of them gave me a look that made my left arm go numb.

"I want a traditional wedding," Leslie said.

"Why?" I inquired. "You've never done anything traditional before, like finish college."

"You always have to bring that up, don't you?"

"I'll make it $3,000," I said.

"Never mind your father, dear," my wife interjected. "You know how he likes to tease."

"Four thousand, but that's my final offer, take it or leave it."

They left it. I should have known. My own wedding did not go as I would have wished. I wanted to drive out into the country like Clark Gable and Claudette Colbert and be married by a justice of the peace who looked like Gene Lockhart. My wife-to-be indicated some willingness for the enterprise, but it was not to be. The mothers got hold of things and before I knew it I was dressed in a white dinner jacket, standing in the vestry of a Baptist Church, listening to a tenor sing "Because."

Someone pushed me out into the aisle, and I remember saying to myself: "I'm an agnostic. I hate ties. I hate that song. What am I doing here in this monkey suit?"

Then my bride appeared in her white gown at the end of the aisle looking incandescent, and I figured it out. A little thing like that can turn your life around.

So Leslie had a traditional wedding—traditional for a backyard ceremony, anyway. Cake, flowers, champagne, a tent, musicians, the whole nine yards—a catered affair. We were spared nothing.

And do you know what? I liked it. It was a gathering of the clan and a few dozen dear friends and it had a warmth to it that stretched back to generations dead and forward to generations yet unborn. It was a meaningful, altogether satisfying ritual.

My favorite part of a wedding is when the minister (we had a chaplain in army dress blues) asks:

"If there be anyone here who knows why this couple should not be joined together in matrimony, let him speak now or foreverafter hold his peace."

It adds just that touch of suspense and excitement that every ritual needs. I hate it when couples make up their own vows and promise to like and respect each other's personhood and take turns doing the laundry.

Sometime after the wedding I was asked if I had any marital advice to give to the newlyweds.

"Yes," I said. "I've always found that marriage goes better if you don't talk to each other before 10 A.M."

"That's it?" Leslie said. "That's the sum total of the wisdom you've gained from twenty-nine years of marriage?"

"It's better than most of the advice you'll get, kid," I replied. My wife gave me a look that numbed my arm again.

The truth is, there is no certain advice to give to the newly married, no tricks that will unlock the secret of eternal happiness. You make a marriage up as you go along. Things come up and you struggle to deal with them. You solve some problems, you learn to live with others, you persevere and, if you're lucky, you prevail.

David and Leslie called up a few days after the wedding and reported that they were amazed at how different it was, being married, and what a nice feeling it was. I took that as a good sign.

I can also report that wedding gifts have changed some since I was married. As I recall we got two toaster ovens, a waffle iron, seventeen sets of bed sheets and 132 bath towels, some of them not marked His and Hers.

Leslie and David got none of those things, not a single toaster oven. They got four electric coffee grinders, four crystal vases, five sets of wine glasses and seven sets of champagne flutes.

"We're going to have to change our lifestyle," David said.

"Yeah," I said, "you're going to have to get one." For which I got another numb left arm as a thank-you.

It really was a beautiful ceremony. Clark Gable and Claudette Colbert will never know what they missed. (1986)

Empty Nest

Autumn is a poignant time for some, a time of loneliness and separation. It is a time when the younger children of the family flutter off to school and the older ones to college, leaving behind them huge gaps of silence.

And when the last one goes off to college, the silence can be deafening. The phone stops ringing, the stereo stops playing obnoxious music and nobody with a funny haircut shows up at the front door any more.

Yes, autumn is a poignant time for some—particularly those who are not playing with a full deck.

I never understood the so-called "empty nest syndrome," that feeling of abject loneliness that afflicts certain parents when their elder children leave home. The kid can be an apprentice ax-murderer, but when he takes off his parents look at each other with tear-filled eyes and say: "The place won't be the same without him."

Personally, I always looked forward to the time when my children would leave home, largely because I knew the place wouldn't be the same without them. Even when they were fairly small I used to give them tips on running away, but they never took them.

Not that I didn't like them, you understand. They were fine children. I would have matched them against any kids you'd care to name, excepting of course those few who showed a talent for making money rather than spending it. The problem was, well, they were kids.

What adult in his or her right mind, given a choice, would choose to live in the close company of teenagers? It's like being occupied by a foreign army. They go days without saying anything intelligible, they take over your favorite part of the house and they break things.

My son, now grown and working in New York, was something of a genius at that part of being a teenager—breaking things. He could break an anvil, provided it was your favorite anvil. And he did it effortlessly, without a trace of surliness or anger. Things just broke in his hand—or under his foot.

I remember one time I bought a styrofoam beer cooler, brought it home and set it down on the floor in the basement. I was straightening up from doing so when he came tumbling downstairs with a "Hi Dad, what's up?" and stuck his foot through the cooler. That was perhaps his quickest performance but by no means his grandest. There were the three cars.

My eldest daughter, also grown and working in New York, was

better at the taking-over part of being a teenager. Books, magazines, umbrellas, sweaters, record players, bath tubs—she'd take them over and make them hers.

She could go into the bathroom for a bath and stay there three days. Generally on the second day my wife would pound on the door until she got a response.

"Please let me alone, I'm taking a bath." That was the response.

"I know, dear," my wife would say, "but your father and I are afraid you'll soften to death."

She shared her record collection with us, I'll give her that. She was always putting a record on the player and saying: "Listen to this. What do you think of it?"

I would respond with something like: "Poor devil. It sounds like a horrible way to die. What was his crime?" But it didn't discourage her. She kept right on playing her records, loud enough to blow out your sinuses.

So I took it quite in stride when our children, one by one, went off to college. I never felt so much we were losing a child as gaining increased access to the refrigerator. Nor was I upset last week when we sent our youngest and cheeriest, Rachel, the college graduate, to seek her fortune. She is the one who once asked for a surgically implanted telephone for Christmas.

Armed with a blithe spirit and an education that cost no more than the Hope Diamond, she loaded her belongings into a bright yellow rented truck and set out for Boston. It was raining.

My first impulse was to break out a case of champagne and celebrate for a week.

We shall miss her. She has a way of entering a house all at once, her spirit reverberating simultaneously in the attic and basement, as well as the living room. "Any calls?" she'd cry as she blew in the door. Usually there were.

We shall miss her at the dinner table, on those rare occasions when she was able to fit us into her busy schedule, with her sly comments on her fellow workers or her siblings. Most of all, I think, we shall miss her laugh. She has a wonderful sense of humor and a ready laugh. We shall miss it a great deal.

But we'll get used to it, as we did with her brother and sister. And they're always welcome to visit, all of them. As Robert Frost once wrote:

"Home is the place where, when you have to go there, they have to take you in."

Young friends, people in their thirties, sometimes ask us whether, if we had it to do over again, we'd have children. I always say, "If you have to ask, you can't afford it."

That's a flip answer, of course. You have children and attempt to shape their lives to your desires and find that they've shaped yours to their needs. They've filled in the cracks with laughter and pain and anxiety and love and formed your lives in a way you would not have predicted nor dared comtemplate.

It's a good and natural thing when they fly off, and the freedom they leave behind is extraordinary. But do it again? Yes. Hell, yes. (1986)

Fights with one's spouse are different from fights with one's children. You can't afford to lose a fight with your husband or wife. Neither can you afford to win.

Ugly Americans

When my wife suggested a vacation to Mexico I said no way. "I don't do Third World countries," I said.

"Mexico isn't a Third World country. It's an emerging industrial nation."

"That means it's a Third World country with air pollution. I don't want to go someplace where the people are conspicuously poor; I'm a liberal. Even less do I want to go where the most famous cultural reward is diarrhea."

"That is a stupid, insensitive, uninformed thing to say. It may even be racist. The culture of Mexico is considerably older and richer than ours. The Mayans were building temples to shame the pyramids when your ancestors were inventing the lard sandwich."

She had me there. I'd overplayed my hand and I knew it. I fought on for a bit, just to keep up appearances, but before long I was stacking suitcases on the front porch, waiting for a ride to the airport. The phone rang. It was our driver; she'd been taken ill.

"See!" I said. "You can't even help someone go to Mexico without getting sick. It's an omen."

"Right," my wife said. "Come on Marco Polo; we'll go to Plan B. Load the luggage in the car. We'll park it at the airport."

I did as I was told. The plane tickets were nonrefundable. Soon we were on our way to Cozumel, an island off the coast of the Yucatan Peninsula in the Caribbean Sea.

The flight was typical for this day and age, much like what a transcontinental bus ride used to be. It was supposed to take seven hours; it took twelve. If you ever want to know anything about the Houston airport, ask me. I've got it memorized.

We finally got to Cozumel. I should have known better than to worry about vacationing in a Third World country. This was not Third World Mexico, it was Tourist Mexico.

Cozumel is one of those apparent paradises that poor countries construct to relieve people from rich countries of superfluous wealth. It is, in most respects, a perfect place. The hotels are modern, the food excellent, the beaches superb, the weather irreproachable and even the water is drinkable, a lot of it. If there is crushing poverty in Cozumel, it is doing its crushing well out of sight of the visitors—almost all American and European—who flock to its shores in enriching hordes.

"This isn't bad," I said to my wife over a Piña Colada after a snorkling session.

"Bad? It's an MGM musical," she said. "All that's missing is the young Judy Garland."

Which, ultimately, is the problem. If you want a nice place in the sun to recover from winter, you can hardly do better than Cozumel. It's lovely. But, it has roughly the same relationship to Mexico as a Chinese restaurant in New York has to China. It offers you the flavor of Mexico—its sights and smells—without requiring you to struggle with the reality of Mexico. You don't have to speak Spanish; people speak English. You don't have to fend off beggars; there are none. You don't have to deal with air pollution; the sky is stunningly blue. The bathrooms are clean, a lot of them.

I began to feel guilty. I'm a liberal.

"I never thought we'd wind up as Ugly Americans," I said to my wife on the third day.

"You're going to ruin this for me, aren't you?" she replied.

"We used to sneer at Americans who would go to foreign countries without speaking the language and stay in hotels filled with other Americans and complain about how they couldn't get a decent hamburger. All that's left for us now is the complaint about the hamburger. We've become the jokes of our youth."

"Oh, yes, you're going to ruin it, I can tell."

"I watched one of the cruise ships come in yesterday. It was filled with old people, people in their sixties and seventies. They came prancing off that white boat, wearing their funny shirts, ready to spend an entire day plumbing the mysteries of Cozumel. They were loaded into buses and driven off somewhere. That's us in ten years; fifteen at the outside."

"I'm getting a headache in my left eye."

"We are to be spared nothing. Pinochle, shuffleboard, charades, we're in for the whole nine yards. I'll bet before we leave here I ask a shopkeeper how much an item costs in real money. I thought middle age was going to be different somehow. I thought we'd be more like William Powell and Myrna Loy."

"I'm going upstairs to the room. When you get this out of your system, you can come up and join me. But not before."

She left and I ordered up a Piña Colada and contemplated the unfairness of life.

That's the trouble with being a liberal. You realize that if life was fair, you wouldn't be doing as well as you are. (1988)

I have always felt deeply those other words of Robert Frost: "Something there is that doesn't like a wall." Also the grass leading up to the wall. That something is me:

Eat Your Heart Out, Luther Burbank

I see where the Cedar Rapids City Council is becoming concerned over the new movement in horticulture—"natural landscaping." As many as 700 people in Cedar Rapids are trying out the concept, and the council is trying to decide whether it's legal. The technique consists of not mowing, allowing the weeds to grow and generally letting your lawn return to prairie, if that's where it came from. It's the latest thing.

I started it.

That's right; I haven't gotten the credit I deserve, but I pioneered the concept of natural landscaping in Iowa. As far back as twenty years ago, I was experimenting with letting weeds grow, not cutting grass and other innovative gardening techniques. The idea—which I called "The Less Is More Philosophy of Landscape Architecture"—came to me in a flash one day while I was edging my lawn in Des Moines.

It was hot and I was sawing away, trying to create a trench between my lawn and the sidewalk, when I suddenly asked myself: "Why am I doing this? The grass is beautiful. The trench is ugly. I am working very hard to make the world an uglier place." So I went inside, had a beer and watched the ball game on television. Thus was natural landscaping born.

Of course, that was only the beginning. I became obsessed with perfecting the technique, and soon my weekends were almost completely taken up with experimentation. First I stopped digging out dandelions and pulling weeds, then I stopped trimming my hedge. I limited my mowing to once a month. I had not yet the courage to stop it altogether; that would come later. I achieved a major breakthrough when I stopped raking my leaves, allowing the wind to blow them around, as nature intended.

I was ahead of my time, of course. My neighbors did not appreciate my great work and not even my wife supported me.

"When are you going to do something about the front yard?" she asked. "It looks like the set for *The Jungle Book* out there!"

"Nonsense, it's really quite beautiful," I told her, "much as it must have been when the red man ruled. You're just not used to it."

"Nobody's used to it. The woman across the street said she lost her two-year-old in our lawn the other day."

"I know the kid. I can't imagine she looked very hard for him."

"The neighbors are getting up a vigilante committee."

"So what are they going to do, burn us out? They can't intimidate me; I'm a renter."

"Which reminds me; the landlord says he's going to evict us unless you start mowing the lawn."

"Now I know how Galileo felt when they tried him for heresy. Must genius always be persecuted?"

"Come on, genius, get moving. Even Galileo caved in, you know."

So I caved in. I hired a kid to mow the lawn.

That ended my most creative period as a natural landscaper, but I still dabbled. One year, I decided that, instead of raking my leaves, I would burn them where they lay. I lived at the cusp of a ravine at the time, and my back yard sloped sharply to a creek. The wind was blowing toward the creek, and I figured that if I set a fire in the leaves at the top of the hill, it would burn down to the creek and stop. Not only would my leaves be taken care of, but the process would probably kill my weeds.

Well, to make a long story short, the wind shifted—in the direction of my neighbor's home. I remember him standing out there, spraying water from his garden hose on the wall of flame as it approached his home and, all the while, shouting obscenities. He was a good sport about it, though. When we moved shortly thereafter, he helped us.

The people of Cedar Rapids who have taken up natural landscaping are having the same problems I did. The neighbors don't understand it; the city council thinks it breeds mosquitoes. It's hard to be on the cutting edge of a movement.

I hope they stick with it, though. It would be nice to think that my work was not in vain. (1981)

6

GOD ISN'T DEAD, SHE'S ONLY SLEEPING

PEOPLE HAVE CALLED me a shallow nincompoop who scratches out a meager living by taking cheap shots at his betters. That's a lie. I'm not that shallow.

To prove it, I occasionally write about the deeper mysteries of life . . . death, sex, God (if any), the meaning of Dan Quayle.

The God question is particularly intriguing. If there is no God, why do so many intelligent people believe in Him? On the other hand, if there is an all-powerful God, why isn't He doing a better job of managing things?

It could very well be that there is a God but He's incompetent. No, that's blasphemous; I retract it. I prefer to believe that if there is a God, He's like my grandmother.

My grandmother was born in the Ukraine. She came here as a young woman, raised a family and retired to her room. During the whole of my childhood, when we all lived in the same house, she stayed in her room.

She did not watch television; there was none. Nor did she listen to the radio. Neither did she read. She simply stayed in her room, raised plants, looked out the window—occasionally clucking in disapproval at what she saw—and thought.

She took an interest in life, but no responsibility for it.

If there is a concept of God that makes sense to me, it is that of an old woman sitting by a window, being vaguely censorious about what's going on, but not doing anything about it.

Out of that sensibility flows these columns, which cover not only God but a whole range of issues that, for want of a better name, we call "values."

I hope that reading them makes you a better person or, if not that, one who is more fun at parties.

In God We Trust?

A couple of weeks ago, the *Register* ran a poll indicating that, of all institutions, Iowans trusted God the most. Leaving aside the question of calling God an institution—which sounds faintly blasphemous to my ear—I have always had grave reservations about the concept of trusting in God. I've never understood just what it is people trust Him to do.

Do we trust Him to make the righteous prosper and the unworthy suffer? Oh, a few old-fashioned Calvinists still believe that, I suppose, but you'd have a hard time documenting the trend. One's personal experience is filled to brimming with examples of scoundrels who live richly in the full sunlight of society's honor and of noble, honest folk for whom life is just one damn thing after another.

Do we trust God to enforce some larger system of order on our miserable lives? Not if, by order, we mean something we can understand. If there is a hallmark to God's interventions in our lives, it is capriciousness. The quintessential act of God is the tornado. It comes swooping down, destroying one man's home, leaving the next untouched. It tears off the wall of a house without disturbing the furniture.

That's life. There may be a divine pattern to it, certainly, but it's difficult to discern while reaping the whirlwind.

Some would argue that it matters not only whether you trust in God, but in which God you trust. There are nearly as many gods as there are religions, and most of them argue for an exclusive franchise. But look at yesterday's paper—people all over the world were getting it in the neck, regardless of race, creed or religion.

The Palestinians were bombing the Israelis, the Israelis the Palestinians; women and children of several faiths were dying. The lobby of a Kansas City hotel collapsed, killing scores of people—most of them Christians, presumably—who were out trying to have a good time. And in China, the Communist God visited His flock with a flood that killed thousands, injured tens of thousands and left hundreds of thousands homeless.

What makes God such an unlikely candidate for trust, it seems to me, is His sense of humor. He's always playing jokes. For example, I'll bet the rains that produced that Chinese flood ended a Chinese drought. I don't know that for sure, but it would be very much in character.

Trustworthy is the last adjective I would apply to God. Awesome, yes. Majestic, certainly. Mysterious, mystifying, unknowable; all of those things. Trust is the gift we offer to God in hopes that He will take it and send the next tornado down the middle of the road instead of into our kitchen. It seems to work for some people, but not for others.

Still, I think that the Iowans who expressed trust in God were closer to the mark than those who favored the second most mentioned institution—the president of the United States. Or the third, the medical profession. The point is, I guess, that a trustworthy institution is hard to find.

Personally, the American institution I trust the most is McDonald's hamburgers. Not that I like them, particularly—I think they taste like cardboard with everything on it—but when you buy a McDonald's you know exactly what you're getting. And it doesn't matter whether you get it in Toledo, Ohio, or Toledo, Spain; it is the same hamburger. That's trustworthiness.

I have a certain limited trust in other things. I trust the Detroit Tigers to finish above at least two teams in their division and below at least two. Only rarely have I been disappointed in this expectation.

I trust Richard Nixon to keep acting out the role of a character in a Dickens novel; the one who disappears early on then, when you've nearly forgotten him, returns essentially unchanged, only richer.

I trust the Pentagon to plead poverty, no matter how much money we feed it.

So you see, I am not totally without trust. But trust in God? No chance. Too unreliable. (1981)

Before we go any further—or farther, as the case may be—perhaps I should tell you my philosophy of life. I think a writer owes a reader that; at least that. There's nothing worse than getting to the end of a book and finding out the author cares what sign you were born under.

This is what I believe, until further notice:

The Power of Negative Thinking

There is a plague sweeping across our land, more virulent than AIDS, more debilitating than television. It is infecting the young as well as the old, the rich and the working poor; everybody, pretty much, except farmers. It is called positive thinking.

You see it everywhere—on Wall Street, in the halls of Congress and in the shops of Main Street; people are bullish on America. Despite the evidence.

Let's face it, we're riding for a fall. We're running huge budget deficits; we're running huge trade deficits; and we're locked in a mad arms race with the Soviet Union, yet people go about their business, cheerful. It's positive thinking I tell you, the curse of the American experiment.

A lot of people think Norman Vincent Peale invented positive thinking. No, he merely named it. Positive thinking is as old as America itself. Native Americans, Indians as we used to call them before our consciousness was raised, were positive thinkers. That's why they thought the white man would let them keep some of the vast continent they inhabited. The Indian gave the white man positive thinking in return for venereal disease and, at the moment, it's hard to know who got the worst of the trade.

I myself, as a youth, was a positive thinker. I'd go around, as chipper as George Bush, thinking positive thoughts. When I'd hear about a hurricane in Florida, I'd think of what a good thing it was for roofers. Did the Mississippi flood? Well, imagine how grateful the people in the Sahara would be for all that water. I was open to all things positive.

Pretty soon I owned two vacuum cleaners, three sets of encyclopedias and an Edsel. I was just about to have aluminum siding put on my brick house when I happened on a book that was to change my life: *The Power of Negative Thinking* by Gerhardt Downer, the Swiss psychologist. Downer was an early disciple of Sigmund Freud but split with the master when he decided that psychoanalysis, while a brilliant concept, was more trouble than being crazy. He moved back to his Alpine village and wrote his masterwork on negative thinking. Its lack of success did not surprise him. His dying words were, "I always knew I'd be a failure."

It was Downer's monumental discovery that, contrary to popular belief, pessimists are happier than optimists. He wrote:

"A pessimist is a person who expects the worst out of any given situation. Ten percent of the time he is wrong and, thus, pleasantly surprised. The other 90 percent of the time he has the satisfaction of saying 'I told you so.'

"An optimist, on the other hand, lives a life of failed expectations. He moves from one disappointment to another, never learning from experience. Also, he owns many sets of encyclopedias."

The philosophy of negative thinking struck me with the force of religious conversion. At last I had found my path through life. I read extensively in Downer's other works: *How to Win Friends Without Keeping Them, The Pursuit of Mediocrity* and *If You Can't Say Something Nice About Someone, Become a Newspaperman.*

It was that last book that was to give form to the rest of my life. It opened the possibility of thinking negatively for a living. I entered the profession of journalism and, after a series of lightninglike failures, was made a columnist. I've hardly had a positive thought since.

It's not as easy as it sounds, actually. Almost anyone can have a negative thought now and then or even for a week at a time. But to consistently think negatively at a high level requires the discipline of a professional.

Over the years I have developed a number of negative-thinking techniques to help me over the smooth spots. Mornings are particularly important. Get off on the right foot in the morning and the next thing you know you're halfway to work, whistling a John Denver tune, unarmed against the day.

To help prevent this, each morning when I arise I go into the bathroom, look into the mirror, and say: "Will this day never end?" That gets me rolling.

There are those who think, mistakenly, that negative thinking leads to depression. Quite the opposite. It is the positive thinker, more often than not, who falls victim to depression when he wakes up to reality.

Which is why I worry about the state the country is in right now. Not since 1929 have we found ourselves in greater need or in shorter supply of negative thinking.

I'd try to tell President Reagan about it, but he probably wouldn't return my call. (1985)

Long-Distance Interview

The current political campaign may have its shortcomings, but a reluctance to delve into profound philosophical questions has not been one of them. Hardly a week has gone by without the American voter being asked to decide on how the universe was created or the nature of the meaning of life and its beginnings. It's been as much a Sunday school as a campaign.

The latest issue to be thrown up by the conflict is whether God hears the prayers of Jews. It has not been raised by either of the candidates, I hasten to add, but by Bible-thumping supporters of Ronald Reagan; most of them fat-faced men who wear white suits and bray pious platitudes into microphones for a living.

Still, it's a serious question, and it deserves serious attention. I feel uniquely qualified to find that answer, for I am neither Christian nor Jew; I am not even an atheist. I am one of those who finds spiritual peace in the moral confusion of Not Being Sure About Things—an agnostic. I oppose abortion on esthetic grounds, I love the Bible as literature, and on the Day of Judgment I shall take notes. Who better to find out whether God hears the prayers of Jews?

I rang up God on the telephone. He answered on the second ring.

"Is that you, God?" I said.

"You were expecting maybe George Burns?" a high, thin voice answered. "Speak your piece, I don't have much time."

"But I thought you had time for everything, even watching the fall of a sparrow."

"That was in the old days, before the invention of pesticides. Now sparrows are falling like flies. The other day a whooping crane dropped dead and I didn't find about it until after the funeral. This is a bigger job than it used to be. What do you want?"

There's a controversy down here, sir. Some people are saying that God doesn't hear the prayers of Jews, that you only hear the prayers of Gentiles. Is that true?"

"What's a Gentile?"

"Well, basically it's someone who isn't a Jew—like a Christian, for example.

"Oy vey, is that all you people have to worry about? Half your planet is starving to death and you're arguing about whether I listen to Christians or Jews?"

"It's a very important matter to some people. If it turns out that you don't hear the prayers of Jews, they're going to vote for Ronald Reagan. If it turns out you do, they'll vote for Jimmy Carter."

"Why is that?"

"I don't know."

"Earth wasn't one of my more successful experiments, you know. Take Mars, for example. Mars has atmosphere, seasons, days, nights, storms, clouds, mountains—just like Earth does—but it never causes me any trouble. I think my mistake with Earth was in creating life."

"Mistake?"

"Sure, I can make a mistake. I'm only superhuman, you know."

"Does that mean you hear the prayers of Jews or don't you?"

"Why shouldn't I hear the prayers of Jews? Some of my best friends are Jews. My son was a Jew for a while. I hear the prayers of everyone—Moslems, Christians, Jews, Buddhists, Zoroastrians, Coptics, Confucians, Hindus, Shintoists and Unitarians. I hear prayers of people who kneel, who stand up, who wear hats, who don't, who whirl, who shake rattles, who hum. I even hear your prayers."

"I don't pray."

"I hear them anyway."

"Is there anyone whose prayers you don't hear?"

"Not really, although there are some whose voices seem to be growing very faint these days."

"Who?"

"Fat-faced men who wear white suits and bray pious platitudes into microphones." (1980)

On Being Secularly Human

I'm generally pretty thick-skinned, but I was cut to the quick last week when that judge in Alabama labeled me a religious nut. Oh, maybe he didn't say that in so many words but he did call secular humanism a religion and, to a card-carrying secular humanist like myself, that's right next-door.

I imagine you're familiar with the case. Federal District Judge Brevard Hand of Mobile, Alabama, ordered some forty-six books removed from Alabama schools because, he ruled, they promoted "secular humanism," thereby violating the Constitution.

"For purposes of the First Amendment," he said, "secular humanism is a religious belief system, entitled to the protection of, and subject to the prohibitions of, the religion clauses. It is not a mere scientific methodology that may be advanced in the public schools." In other words, the lack of religious instruction in the schools itself constitutes a kind of religion.

If that seems a little bizarre one must remember that Judge Hand is a Nixon appointee. I'm sure he's doing the best he can. But I'm here to say that he's wrong. Secular humanism is not a religion; it's hardly even a philosophy. It's more of an ideological lean-to that serves as shelter for the cosmically bewildered. Ask your average secular humanist one of the more important religious questions, like: "What does it all mean?" and he is apt to answer with a shrug and an "I don't know." Secular humanists use the shrug like Catholics use genuflection.

They do not have a uniform, a priesthood, an orthodoxy or bake sales. They do not burn people at the stake, canonize them or argue whether the Pope is infallible or merely a good guesser. So where's the religion?

Secular humanists come in all shapes and sizes—some even believe in God—but they are bound by the belief that it is possible to construct a system of right and wrong without reference to divine wisdom which is, in any case, inscrutable. It has its roots in the Italian Renaissance, that unparalleled flowering of human genius in the fifteenth and sixteenth centuries. It is an intellectual, rather than spiritual, movement. If Mother Teresa's spiritual life can be compared to the Sistine ceiling, the spiritual life of a typical secular humanist can be compared to a picture post card. You turn it over and it says: "Having a wonderful time. Wish you were here."

I don't apologize for that. It works. Christianity is a profoundly beautiful religion, but its effect on deportment is not as great as Christians would have us believe. If all you knew about people was whether they were Christian or heathen, you'd have a tough job separating the good guys from the bad guys.

Actually, I've always thought that humanists had a moral advantage over those who believe in reward and punishment after death. It's easy to do the right thing if you think you'll suffer the eternal hellfires of damnation for doing wrong. Humanists do the right thing simply because it's right.

Still not convinced?

Imagine a Martian making a guided tour of the planet Earth. His guide explains Christianity to him.

"What a wonderful religion," he says. "How very daring to base conduct on love and self-sacrifice—how touching. It seems a demanding philosophy, however. Is it very popular?"

"Oh, yes," the guide replies. "Many of the most civilized countries of the planet are Christian countries." "That's very encouraging," the Martian says. "You are lucky to have so many countries committed to love and peace and brotherhood. It must be a very tranquil planet. Tell me something of its recent history."

And the guide begins to relate the history of the twentieth century—a story of brutal serial wars, monstrous destruction and wholesale murder, much of it done by Christians against Christians. At which point the Martian says:

"Would you explain Christianity to me again. I think I missed something."

Still, Judge Hand's ruling wasn't all bad. The textbooks he threw out were awful; at least the ones that were written about. They did not merely fail to promote religion, they all but ignored it. They did not mention, for example, the religious motivation of the Pilgrims and the fact that Martin Luther King was a minister. That's not secular humanism, that's dumb.

I, for one, would be happy to see religion taught in the schools, taught as I would like to see all subjects taught—analytically, critically, in a historical context and with a sense of humor. And not just Christianity. Our students should be told something of all the world's great religions. But that probably wouldn't satisfy the right-wingers. You just can't please some people. (1987)

Armaggedon and Pisgah

You can sleep a little more soundly in your beds tonight, folks. Even if the Rooskies come over with their missiles, raining warheads down on us in a nuclear hailstorm, you don't have to worry about a thing. The government has a plan. An escape plan.

People in Cedar Falls will go to Mason City. Those in Indianola will flee to Albia. And, as a special treat, people in Council Bluffs will be encouraged to go to Pisgah.

No, I'm not kidding; would I joke about a nuclear holocaust? I read about the plan in last Sunday's *Register,* so it's official.

The federal government is leaning on Iowa's eight largest cities— and on cities throughout the nation, for that matter—to develop evacuation plans in case of a nuclear attack.

A nuclear war with the Soviet Union would kill about 180 million of us, civil-defense officials say, but if we got good at emptying our cities into the countryside, we could save as many as fifty million of those lives.

And if you believe that, I've got some land in Arizona I'd like you to buy sight unseen.

The trouble with trying to plan one's response to nuclear war is that, to do so, you have to scale it down to human size. We tell ourselves it's a lot like World War II, but with bigger explosions. That's absolute nonsense, of course. A nuclear war will make World War II look like a block party.

If the balloon goes up, it is going to be so much bigger, so much more destructive, so much more terrible than anything we have ever known that our minds recoil at realistic contemplation of it. A nuclear war will not merely kill people, it will shred people, crush people, fry people, melt people, vaporize people, suffocate people—and to those to whom it does none of those things, it will give cancer. And our answer to this is Pisgah?

You've got to be kidding.

My family has a plan to be carried out in case of nuclear attack; I developed it myself.

First of all, when we hear word of World War III we shall—all of us—try our very best to get home as quickly as we can. Once there, we shall light a fire in the fireplace, put some nice music on the record player and drink the best wine we have in the house.

In short, we shall attempt to meet the ultimate horror with a sense of grace and civility.

I don't know whether we'll be able to accomplish this, of course—the odds are against it—but we shall try. And to that end, we practice the drill as often as we can. It's got as good a chance of working as the evacuation plan.

Given a few minutes to live, I should hope I would try to live them as well as possible, not in a traffic jam on the road to Pisgah. (1981)

Out of the Closet

The *Register*'s recent series on homosexuality in Iowa has provoked a storm of controversy. I'm not surprised. Homosexuals and fat people are about the last groups left regarding whom God-fearing, right-thinking people can pursue bigotry without experiencing guilt and the contempt of polite society.

True, I was a little unprepared for the virulence of the reaction—

Iowa generally being a paragon of moderation—but I suppose that figures too. We have engaged in a conspiracy of silence about homosexuality for so long that it has assumed a kind of mythic status that touches subterranean fears. "The love that dare not speak its name," that sort of thing. I myself have not talked much about the subject.

So maybe it's time I did, fully and frankly. I have a confession to make.

I am a homo-indifferent.

I admit it; I don't care whether a person is homosexual, heterosexual or sexual. There! I've said it and I'm glad. And I'm not just saying that, either. I mean I *really don't care.*

That would be bad enough, but there's more. I don't think homosexuals are evil, perverted, immoral or even unnatural. I believe them to be, at worst, mildly unusual, like people who are left-handed.

As long as I'm confessing, I might as well go all the way. It gets worse yet. I don't see anything wrong with homosexual marriage; that is, a legal acknowledgment by society of a relationship between consenting adults.

And you know how the Scriptures say it's a sin to be a homosexual? I think the Scriptures are wrong.

These are terrible admissions, I know, but I can't help it. It's the way I feel.

It wasn't that I was brought up wrong. Growing up in my Polish neighborhood on the near-northwest side of Detroit, I was as homophobic as you'd want. I made jokes about queers and faggots and laughed at limp-wristed impersonations, just like the other guys.

But then I made the mistake of going to college where I fell in with bad company—writers. Worse yet, I met some homosexuals. I found I liked them. (That's the danger of actually meeting people who are members of groups you hate. They very often turn out to be likable.) They were, for the most part, smart, witty, warm, generous people who, I later learned, make terrific friends; at least the ones I met did. Gradually I began to question my prejudice. I began to ask myself: what did I care what they did when the lights went out? And even if I did care, what business was it of mine?

I've never found an adequate answer to those questions and until I do I'm going to maintain my homo-indifference. (Gee, this confessing feels good. Maybe I can get a guest shot on "The Oprah Winfrey Show." "Donahue," even.)

Now that I've come out of the closet I may become a sexually indifferent activist. Probably not, though. Not everyone is cut out for indifference. If your life is so free of problems that you have time to delve into the intimate lives of strangers or if you are so sure that you are doing everything just right that you feel comfortable in instructing others on how to deal with their most profound feelings, then you probably should, for you are indeed a godlike creature.

If, on the other hand, you are like most of us and suffer from intermittent feelings of confusion and doubt in matters both sexual and spiritual, then perhaps some benign neglect might be called for.

You know, the older I get, the less I know what "normal" is. I look at my friends, most of whom have made modest successes of their lives, and none of them seems normal to me; that is, they don't do things the way I do them.

I have one friend who, though a journalist of national reputation and handsome income, wears nothing but secondhand clothes. I have another who, though well into middle age, spends an inordinate amount of his income on bicycles. Another walks the edge of poverty to support a boating habit. The other week I met a young man, married with children, who is deliberately living below the poverty line so that he won't have to pay taxes to fuel this country's war machine.

None of these people are normal. And that's with the lights on! Who knows what baroque fantasies they act out in the dark? For that matter, who knows what sexual demons bedevil the Bible-thumping preachers who cry out against the sin of homosexuality from the pulpits of Iowa each Sunday?

Not that I care. I stand in this matter with Mrs. Patrick Campbell who said:

"It doesn't matter what you do in the bedroom as long as you don't do it in the street and scare the horses."

I hope my shameful admission doesn't make you think ill of me, but if it does, it does. There comes a time in a person's life when he can no longer deny his true nature, and mine is passionately indifferent. (1990)

Dirty Pictures

Hang on to your chastity belts folks, the Federal Communications Commission is going to save us from ourselves again.

Last week the FCC announced its intention to ban all "indecent" programming on radio and television, everywhere except cable television. Under the proposal, which still has to be approved by a federal court, a radio or television station that violated the twenty-four-hour-a-day ban on smut could be fined.

It's being done for the children's sake, of course. Officials said the action was taken in response to a growing public feeling that young, impressionable minds should be shielded from vulgar and otherwise questionable material.

"Parents feel beleaguered in their efforts to instill proper values," said one of the commissioners, citing "a public outcry against indecency and obscenity."

And if the commission has a difficult time defining "indecency" with precision, be assured that it will know it when it sees it.

While I have nothing against protecting the minds of children—although politicians crying out against indecency run a serious risk of being struck by lightning—the FCC is barking up the wrong antenna. It's not the indecency on radio and television that's destroying the minds of the young, it's the decency.

It's the game shows, the soap operas, the mindless sitcoms, the endless sports programming, the celebrity talk shows and, most of all, the commercials that are turning the minds of our young into mush. Radio isn't any better, but it is less effective.

Ninety percent of what appears on television could win the Good Housekeeping Seal of Approval, but its effect is as poisonous as the most vile pornography. Television has reduced several generations of our children to slack-jawed zombies who know neither physical exercise nor intellectual stimulation.

It is as if a foreign power had defeated us in a war and, seeking to render us quiescent, subjected us to television. And it worked.

Perhaps you think I exaggerate. Last week the Times-Mirror Center for the People and the Press issued a report, based on extensive research, saying that the current generation of young people "knows less, cares less, votes less and is less critical of its leaders and institutions than young people in the past . . .

"Over most of the past five decades, younger members of the public have been at least as well informed as older people," the study found. "In 1990 that is no longer the case."

The trend is reflected most dramatically in voting patterns, where the percentage of people between the ages of eighteen to twenty-four who vote is less than half of that of the forty-five to sixty-four age group.

There are a variety of reasons for that discrepancy, of course, but none so dominant as television. The mind is a computer, after all, and you know what they say about computers: garbage in, garbage out.

There are two terrible things about television:

• **There's a lot of it**—The stories you read about kids watching thirty, forty, and fifty hours of television a week are terrifying to one who takes the future of the country seriously. What can their parents be thinking of? Watching fifty hours of commercial television a week is enough to turn a chimpanzee into a goldfish. Hell, it's turning our kids into goldfish. Parents who allow their children unrestricted use of the television set should be arrested for child abuse.

• **It comes in very small pieces**—The content of your average television show would be bad enough, but it arrives in snippets and dribbles. A few seconds of this, a few seconds of that, then on to the next thing. This is especially true of network television news where quotes are seldom longer than thirteen words and camera shots aren't held beyond three seconds. Television news is like trying to read a newspaper written on confetti. The effect of this, over years, is to shorten the attention span of the viewer until it becomes impossible for him or her to concentrate on anything longer than a few seconds.

You do that for a few generations and you wind up with an electorate that can't absorb any political message that can't be stated in a thirty-second commercial, most of it pictures.

It doesn't make for a dumb nation, exactly, but after a while it might as well be. That's the road we're traveling.

If the FCC wants to protect the young it shouldn't ban indecency on television, it should ban television.

I know, that goes too far; I'm a dreamer. The airwaves are public property, however, and when we rent them out we have a right to expect something back for it.

Something besides brain-dead children. (1990)

Villains

The paper recently carried a story about college faculty members at Catholic University choosing a list of ten great villains of history. It was a bad list. Attila the Hun, Hitler, Stalin, Caligula, Nero—like that. Dull. What's the sense of going to the trouble of making up a list that a seventh-grader could come up with?

The list wasn't even altogether successful on its own terms; it included Mao Tse-tung, who some would say was a great improvement over his predecessor, but it ignored Torquemada, the Spanish monk who is credited with burning more than 10,000 persons to death during the Inquisition. I guess they figured that Torquemada, while authoritarian, was not totalitarian, but that Mao was.

There are more interesting and instructive lists to be made. Mark Twain once expressed the belief that Benjamin Franklin was one of history's great villains. Citing the unfortunate example Franklin set for youngsters, Twain wrote:

"With a malevolence which is without parallel in history, he would work all day and then sit up nights and let on to be studying algebra by the light of the smoldering fire so that all other boys might have to do that also or else have Benjamin Franklin thrown up to them."

A friend once had a professor who thought that the two greatest villains of history were Winston Churchill and Dale Carnegie. "Churchill made war noble and Carnegie, the handshake false," he said.

Those are interesting villains. In that spirit, I would like to offer my own list of great villains of modern times. For example:

• **Ivy Lee**—The man who, early in the century, persuaded John D. Rockefeller to give away dimes to children, thus inventing public relations.

• **Joyce Kilmer**—In writing "Trees," he ruined poetry for generations of Americans. No wonder Americans don't like poetry; they think "Trees" is a poem.

• **Henry Ford**—He made it possible for virtually everyone to own a car, thereby paving the way.

• **Billy Graham**—He made an emotional, Bible-thumping style of evangelism respectable, setting the stage for such charlatans and mountebanks as Jerry Falwell, Jim Bakker, Pat Robertson and the Ayatollah Khomeini.

• **Henry Luce**—He founded *Time* magazine, starting the publishing empire that culminated in *People* magazine, perhaps the only national publication that can lay claim to being dumber than television.

• **Dwight Eisenhower**—He failed to kick Richard Nixon off the Republican ticket in 1952 after the "Checkers" speech, which not only gave us almost twenty-five years of Nixon, it dealt a blow to intelligent political speech-making from which it has not yet recovered.

• **Vince Lombardi**—As football coach of the Green Bay Packers, he popularized a cruel code of honor that emphasized stoicism above sportsmanship. While this was more or less appropriate to the crass and brutal game he coached, it was picked up by countless brainless coaches and applied to generations of suffering schoolboys.

• **J. Edgar Hoover**—He single-handedly gave law enforcement a bad name.

• **Alexander Graham Bell**—The inventor of the telephone, an instrument of torture that has made communication between people virtually impossible.

• **Levi Strauss**—He invented designer jeans.

• **Phyllis Schlafly**—Who has been able to strike damaging blows to the concept of the equality of women that no man could have managed. She is the quisling of the women's movement, the president of Vichy Feminism.

• **William Paley**—As the guiding force behind CBS, he was the first one to figure out that people will watch anything if it's free, even commercials.

• **John Wayne**—He spent a lifetime promoting a bogus image of America that now seems to have become the basis of United States foreign policy. (1981)

Love Story

Another romantic myth died the other day, a victim of the *New York Times*.

For the past ten years or so, the African rhinoceros has been under an assault by hunters that threatens to drive it into extinction. The reason for this, according to myth, was that the rhino horn was highly valued as an aphrodisiac, particularly in Asian countries. And the reason for this, I was told, was due to the rhino's mating habits.

In contrast to most animals, who mate quickly, almost in a perfunctory manner, the rhino's style can only be described as deliberate. The rhino's mating process, it seems, can take a half hour or more. From this grew the idea that the horn of a rhino, ground to powder, might prove helpful in human affairs of the heart. I never tried to verify the story, I simply chose to believe it.

Well, the other day, the *New York Times* blew the myth to smithereens. It turns out that the rhino horn is not particularly valued as an aphrodisiac in the Orient and that the rhino is being threatened not by human passion but by the price of oil.

Apparently it is the custom in South Yemen for the men to wear daggers that are given them in a ritual that signals the reaching of manhood. Daggers are as common there as neckties are on Wall Street. The preferred material for the handles of these ceremonial daggers is the horn of the rhinoceros.

Until the early 1970s, South Yemen was a poor country in which few people could afford the relatively expensive rhino model dagger. But when OPEC was formed and petroleum prices shot up, Yemenis found lucrative work in the oil fields of Saudi Arabia and the Persian Gulf states and began sending their money home.

Buoyed by this new prosperity, Yemenis started buying top-of-the-line daggers. The price of rhino horn rose to the demand, and poachers started shooting the lumbering beast in unprecedented numbers. It is believed that the rhino population of Africa was cut in half during the 1970s, and it continues to fall.

I am against the extinction of the rhino under any circumstances—it would be a tragic loss if such an outrageous beast were to disappear from the planet—yet I'd feel better about it if I thought it was for a good cause. But ceremonial daggers?

That's the trouble with romantic illusion; it seldom can stand the harsh light of reality.

A half hour. Or more. (1982)

More Bad News

I was remarking to a friend the other day that it had been years since I'd seen a skywriter; you know, those airplanes that drew messages in white smoke across the sky; advertising messages, mainly. We used to see them all the time during the summer when I was a kid. We'd stand there while the pilot laboriously spelled out the letters of his slogan, and we'd try to guess what he was going to say before he'd finish. P . . . E . . . P . . . S . . .

In my neighborhood, some guys couldn't guess it until the "C."

Well, the other day, I saw skywriting done 1980s style—five planes, zooming across the sky, leaving little puffs of smoke that formed themselves into letters. They spelled out "In Washington Summertime Means Miller Time" in about three minutes. They don't each pick a letter or anything; they simply fly wing to wing, leaving these puffs of smoke that become words.

It was amazing, but it still left me a little nostalgic for the days when you could spend an hour and a half watching a skywriter lazily practicing his art.

The rhino is going, the old-fashioned skywriters are gone; sooner or later, we're going to live in a world where nothing takes longer than three minutes.

Terminating with Extreme Prejudice

Let's talk about capital punishment. Everyone else is. The execution of Steve Judy last week seems to have set off the debate again. Columnist George Will wrote that Judy's crime—which consisted of raping and killing a motorist who stopped to help him, then drowning her three small children in a creek—"should stir doubts in those opponents of capital punishment whose minds are not closed as tight as eggs."

Let it never be said that I went through life with a mind closed to the beneficence of capital punishment.

I've never been totally opposed to it, in any case. A man takes a life and his is taken in return. There's a certain Biblical symmetry to that. It's the detail work that gets messy.

For example, whom do you kill and why? How do you do it?

If you're trying, literally, to "punish" someone for a heinous act, then killing him is a poor way. Punishment, to be most effective, must be experienced, and capital punishment by its very nature is over even as it begins. In punishing the criminal, it puts him beyond punishment. It makes no sense.

If, on the other hand, you are seeking to remove people like Steve Judy from society, then killing them is a good way. There are other good ways, but none quite so definitive as execution. The only problem—and it's a quibble—is with the name. Why call it capital punishment when what you're really doing is conducting an extermination? Perhaps we might borrow the CIA's ironic bureaucratese for semi-official executions: "Termination with Extreme Prejudice."

The crux of the argument for capital punishment, however, is that it acts as a deterrent to people who would otherwise be moved to commit capital crimes.

There's some truth in that; not, perhaps, with demented sadists like Judy or Charles Manson, but the hands of hold-up men and the like might be stayed by the threat of execution.

Once you accept the deterrent argument, however, it is unconscionable to insist that the execution be carried out in the privacy of a prison garage. If you're holding up execution as an example of the kind of bad thing that can happen to bad people, you want as many people as possible to see it and be deterred. There's no getting around it: The state should televise executions on public television in prime time.

Of course, there's always the danger of making a Jimmy Cagney movie out of the process and turning the creeps and bums on death row into public heroes, but it's a risk we would have to take. Televised executions are central to the deterrent value of capital punishment.

The method of execution presents interesting moral, esthetic and practical problems. I reject out of hand the gas chamber which, whatever its virtues, is too vivid a reminder of the martyrdom of innocent millions.

Romantic that I am, I have a soft spot in my heart for the guillotine, with its long and proud history, but I'm afraid we would find it a trifle French for our tastes. And then there's the blood.

Hanging is a more traditionally American way of death, but for all of its undeniable theatricality, it is a brutal, erratic means of dispatching the unworthy. Literature is filled with horror stories of things gone wrong at hangings—up to and including an occasional head being torn from an occasional overweight body.

A firing squad has its points. Certainly it's dramatic enough, but it would make us seem a little like a banana republic, don't you think?

All things considered, I'm for the electric chair. It's a sinister looking contraption, for one thing, something you can point out to children and say:

"See? See? If you don't behave, they're going to strap you into that and—zap!" It has been tried and tested over the years, and it has kind of an American feel to it. I don't think we could do better.

Of course, it's not energy-efficient and, in these troubled times, you could get into trouble with conservation groups.

Which is the real argument against capital punishment, I suppose. There's no way to do it well. (1981)

But if you must have capital punishment—and it does seem to be an idea whose time has come, again—you at least try to make it an effective instrument of deterence, one that persuades other potential criminals to suppress their worst instincts. To that end, you should target not dope dealers, who have a life expectancy of six months in any case, but classes of criminals who are planning to live forever: bankers, lawyers, doctors and government bureaucrats.

For example, we are now in the midst of the greatest financial scandal in the history of our nation. Through a combination of avarice and ineptitude, not to mention corruption, savings and loan executives have looted their institutions of hundreds of billions of dollars over the past few years. Yes, hundreds of billions. American taxpayers are expected to make good on this theft, which they will do uncomplainingly because they do not understand the situation; they are too busy worrying about more important things, like Donald Trump's broken marriage.

A few of the sleazy operators might go to jail for a while but, for the most part, they shall slip through our loose nets of justice to enjoy the fruits of their labors. The deterrent to future corruption will be nil.

But if you hanged one or two of them—a half dozen at the outside—the salutary effect on his or her colleagues would be stunning. They would recalibrate the risk of doing shady business and we might, in time, again deposit our funds in a federal institution with the certain knowledge that they would be there when we reached for them.

Lawyers pose a tougher problem, not only because there are so many of them but because it is difficult to draw a distinction between criminal activity and what they do normally. It is a lawyer's job, after all, to find that thin line between that which is barely permissible and that which is felonious and to walk that line. And he is honor-bound to pursue his client's interests to his client's last red cent.

Still, when a lawyer crosses that line—for example, by plundering the estate of an elderly widow—it would be well to hang him. Several hundred hangings would do more for the ethics of the profession than all the canons in all the law schools in all the world.

Some might argue that executing doctors for their mistakes is overly harsh. Why? They execute us for ours, the most common one being choosing the wrong doctor. Damn me for an innocent, but I think a well-placed execution or two would make doctors more careful. At the very least it might make them lower their fees.

Bureaucrats are far less controversial targets. Who could argue that government could not be made more efficient, more honorable and, yes, kinder and gentler, if former HUD Secretary Sam Pierce were made to climb the gallows? It's self-evident. As a matter of fact Herbert Hoover, while president, suggested that he be allowed to hang a bureaucrat of his choice once a month to set an example for the rest. His was a much underappreciated intellect.

There are other groups that might profit from capital punishment—bad drivers, shoppers who get in the express check-out line with thirteen items in their carts, people who talk in movies, video club members who fail to rewind the tapes before they return them— but I'm perfectly willing to stick with a few major offenders to begin with. Then, if it proves effective, we can branch out.

In any case, we don't want to be too severe. We're not drug czars, after all. (1990)

Safe Sex

So they're talking about condoms right out loud these days, on the television even. That, to one of my advanced years, is almost shocking. When I was a boy we never uttered the C-word in polite society. It was a subject left to the braggadocio of the locker room or gas station.

You certainly never used "condom" in mixed company or in cross-generational conversations. Not by word or deed would you ever indicate to your parents that you so much as knew the word, and they reciprocated in kind.

Actually buying a condom back then was a dreadful experience. You'd go into a drug store and wait around at the magazine rack until the druggist, the elderly one, was alone at the counter. Then you'd steal over, lean forward and, in a low voice, say: "Could I have a package of condoms, please?" You always half-expected the druggist to shout back: "WHAT DO YOU WANT CONDOMS FOR, SONNY?" He never did, but the threat was there. He had to reach below the counter to get them, and he passed them over like contraband.

Today condoms are displayed on open shelves in supermarkets, and the great argument is whether we should allow them to be advertised on television. That's how far we've progressed. Or fallen.

It's AIDS that's done it, of course. Teenage pregnancy gets some credit, but young girls have been getting pregnant for a long time and nobody ever suggested advertising condoms on television before. AIDS, until now a disease primarily of homosexuals and drug users, has broken into the heterosexual population and promises to advance through it relentlessly in the coming years. Given the grim nature of the disease, that is truly a terrifying prospect.

The solution of some, liberals mainly, is to promote the use of condoms as a way of avoiding the disease. The solution of others, conservatives mainly, is to promote sexual abstinence.

Being a liberal, I favor the first method, even at the cost of using television to do it. (Television networks, gathering their dignity about them like a Victorian lady her shawl, thus far have refused to run condom ads. Bad taste, they say. Those guys are so noble, you wonder how they ever make any money.)

But I can see the point of those who would adopt the "Don't do it" approach. They feel that you really can't promote the use of condoms among the young without promoting sexual activity as well. "If you can't be good, be careful" was not one of the messages on Moses' tablet, is their feeling, and there's some truth to that.

I have, however, a reassuring anecdote for those people. It is a personal anecdote.

It happened when I was in college, about nineteen years old and wholly innocent. I had never even gotten close enough to a girl to find out whether I was shy.

Some friends and I got an invitation to a dance at a nearby Catholic girls school. My secular humanist heart soared. A Catholic girls school! Virginal maidens waiting for a sophisticated college lout to unlock their passion! I could see myself at the dance, enticing an Audrey Hepburn look-alike to rapture. We'd steal away together to a private place and then . . .

I went out and bought a package of condoms. Before we left I slipped one into my trouser pocket.

We were greeted at the school door by a nun who looked like Vince Lombardi, only less cheerful. She inspected us with obvious disapproval, then called our blind dates on the phone and announced our presence. We young men stood around in the lobby, hands in pockets, rehearsing nonchalance. The young ladies arrived—nice looking girls—and approached. I took my hand out of my pocket to greet my date and as I did so . . . yes . . . the condom fell out. On the tile floor. With an amazingly loud slap. I remember staring at it for a long moment as though hypnotized. Then I stepped on it, covering it with my foot.

It was a near tragedy. My friends almost suffered brain damage. Two of them turned remarkable shades of blue, trying not to laugh. The third rushed out of the building, doubled up.

The girls seemed confused at the scene, encouraging me to believe they hadn't seen the condom or, perhaps, had not recognized it for what it was. The nun was less encouraging. I bent down and pretended to tie my shoe, taking the opportunity to retrieve the condom. The fact that I was wearing shoes with buckles didn't help matters.

It was a long, dismal evening. My date and I never got out of the full glare of Sister Lombardi's vigilance. On the way home I threw the still-packaged condom into a snow bank. So you see, even the *sale* of condoms doesn't always guarantee sexual activity.

Condoms don't cause sex, people do. Or don't. (1987)

7

WINNING ISN'T THE ONLY THING; THERE'S LOSING, FOR EXAMPLE

THIS COUNTRY HAS been ga-ga about sports since the 1920s at least, but not until football found television and vice versa did we go over the edge. The two were ideally mated to embody the American spirit—violence in the service of commerce. It was a marriage made in heaven; if not heaven, Disneyland. We are now a nation whose Sunday afternoons in the fall are committed to watching short bursts of brutality interspersed with long interludes of salesmanship.

Far be it from me to suggest that They use sports to distract Us from what They keep doing to Us; or point out that the more we watch sports, the less we vote. I'm not some kind of a nut, you know.

It's difficult to remember at this distance, but there was a time when Americans actually played games as well as watched them. Boys would spend their summer days in pickup games of baseball in vacant lots. When that got old, there was touch football. A person of more or less human dimension could try out for his school team with some expectation of success.

No more. Athletics are now given over to the huge and talented; the rest of us watch.

It's a pity because the very real lessons of sports—sacrifice, dedication, sportsmanship—are virtually lost to the spectator. A good deal of what I know today I learned from the games I played when I was a kid.

Pinball, for example. What you learned from pinball was how to cheat. Your parents, teachers, your minister—none of whom could be trusted for accurate information on important matters—all told you that "cheaters never win." Anyone who took the trouble to look around knew that was a lie; you could see any number of cheaters prospering above their moral superiors. And so long as they didn't get caught, they continued to prosper to the grave, if not beyond.

Pinball gave one instruction in the art of cheating. You could improve your score by jiggling the machine, but if you got greedy and jiggled too much, the machine would register a "TILT," and your game would be canceled out. It was very character-building.

Then there was pool. The thing you learned in pool was the value of not showing off. If you went into a pool hall and immediately began to play as well as you were able, you faced disaster. The other players would take your measure and those who weren't as good would stay away. The only ones you could get a game with were those confident of taking your money. The trick was to play with modesty, encouraging players of lesser skill into a game with you so you could take their money.

Pool also taught you not to gloat after a victory obtained by the above method, lest you suffered the pool player's occupational hazard—broken thumbs.

Perhaps the greatest of educational games, however, was poker. It taught you to greet good fortune and bad with the same face and to make the best of what's given to you. If you were lucky, it also taught you to quit while you were ahead.

And through it all ran the common thread, that things are seldom what they seem. A person who has mastered that lesson is a rich person indeed.

More apt to vote, anyway.

The Mystery of Football

Bear Bryant died last week, plunging the state of Alabama into a depression from which it may never recover; which only proves that there is hardly an event, no matter how sad, that does not have some cheerful aspect.

Don't misunderstand me. I do not make light of Mr. Bryant's death, nor that of any man, but it seems to me that the public response to his final time-out is a bit overwrought. He was not Franklin

D. Roosevelt or Albert Einstein or Jackie Robinson, after all—someone who made a great difference in the life of his country. He was a football coach; not more, not less.

True, he won a lot of games, something over three hundred more than any coach before him (unless you count all of Amos Alonzo Stagg's victories), but that was the limit of his contribution to the game. Stagg was much the greater coach, certainly, regardless of how you count his wins. He invented virtually everything worth inventing about football: the huddle, for example.

Think of that. What would football be without the huddle? Why, nothing. The huddle is the most important part of football. It takes up virtually the entire game.

The Super Bowl is being played today. The game will take approximately two and a half hours. Of that time, the ball will actually be in play for about nine minutes. Most of the rest of the time the game will be taken up with huddles. And the team that huddles best will win, mark me.

And yet, for all its importance, you never hear huddles mentioned by so-called football experts. The Super Bowl today has a two-hour pregame show. It will be filled with analyses of the two teams, the Miami Dolphins and the Washington Redskins. You will hear about which team has the best offense, defense, passing, rushing, pass rush, punting, field goal kicking, punt returning; which team runs the best pass patterns, even.

Have you ever watched someone run a pass pattern? He runs from the line of scrimmage a few yards, then turns left or right. Sometimes he goes straight. That's a pass pattern. But you will hear them analyzed today.

What you will not hear is one word about huddles, the most important part of the game. Not only that: During the game there won't be a single slow-motion, stop-action, instant replay of a huddle—not one.

To my mind, the greatest football coach of all time, after Stagg, was Red Sanders of UCLA. He was a master of the huddle. His teams used to leave their huddles single-file in a serpentine line, arranged so that the players would arrive at the line of scrimmage in their proper position. It was a remarkable thing to watch, and it generally mesmerized the other team's players. They'd just stand there and watch it in awe and admiration. You could see the life go out of them. "What chance do we have against a team that huddles like that?" they seemed to say. Sanders teams won almost all the time. Everybody thought it was because they played such a classy single-wing, but really it was their huddles.

With the single exception of chess, football is the only game in the world where the players spend 85 percent of their time trying to figure out what to do next. It is the huddle that gives the game its uniquely American character. The French don't play football because they can't have a huddle without an argument. There are other reasons foreign countries don't play football, of course.

The Italians don't play it because their quarterbacks can't give signals without using their hands.

The Germans don't play it because every time the players cross the goal line they try to invade the stands.

The Israelis don't play it because they want to defend both end zones, which, according to their interpretation of the Bible, they have a right to settle.

The English almost play football—they call it rugby—but they have been unable to master the huddle. They have something called a scrum, which is a huddle with punching, hardly conducive to contemplation.

They'll probably have a moment of silence for Bear Bryant at the game today; they always have a moment of silence for something. Which is fine.

But during that moment, my mind will turn to thoughts of Amos Alonzo Stagg, without whom there would be no Super Bowl. Not one longer than ten minutes, anyway. (1983)

The Sweet Science

They billed the Mike Tyson-Michael Spinks go as the Fight of the Century (boxing being what it is, there is a Fight of the Century every six months), but it was better than that. It was the quintessential sporting event of the decade.

No other athletic contest has so captured the spirit of the 1980s; its greed, its sense of self-importance, its lack of intrinsic worth. It got about as much publicity as World War II, made as much money as Switzerland, was over in ninety-one seconds and Donald Trump was the host. Perfect.

We live in an age when television yo-yos like Geraldo Rivera can mesmerize a nation by not finding treasure in a vault; bimbos like Vanna White can become famous by memorizing the alphabet; the junk in Andy Warhol's attic brings $15 million; Sylvester Stallone can make hundreds of millions starring in the same picture over and over again; and the president governs by indifference. Even Halley's Comet was a no-show. In that environment, Tyson-Spinks was a classic.

Ninety-one seconds! Soft boiled eggs take longer than that. Take longer, hell; they're more interesting than that.

I must confess that I was influenced by the hype; I thought Spinks would do better. Tyson's battered but beautiful wife does better than that, why shouldn't Spinks? He was the world champion of something or other, after all. He was, supposedly, crafty.

More crafty than we knew, perhaps. It looked as though Spinks went out there saying: "I'm going to make thirteen mill tonight no matter what. Please, God, let me leave the ring healthy enough to enjoy it." Then the bell rang and he took the matter out of God's hands.

I can relate to that. Courage consists of overcoming fear. Intelligence often consists of giving in to it. The best places in the cemetery are reserved for the brave. The best places in the better retirement communities, however, are filled by the wise.

Spinks made roughly $150,000 a second for his performance. For that kind of money, I'd fight Tyson. I mean it. I can see it now, the ring announcer comes to the microphone and begins the introductions:

"And in this corner, on his knees praying, wearing bicycle shorts, weighing 180 pounds, 164 when he's in shape, the undefeated contender, Don (The Rabbit) Kaul."

And when my handlers hauled me to my feet and hurled me into the center of the ring, I would touch gloves with Tyson, then throw myself on my back and refuse to get up. I could make a million and a half dollars just being counted out. That, basically, is what Spinks did, but, out of pride, he let Tyson hit him once to give him an excuse for fainting. I would simply eliminate the subterfuge.

I know what you're thinking; no one would pay to see me swoon before Mike Tyson. Nonsense. It's all in the selling. I would be billed as the Walter Mitty contender who's discovered the secret of disguising muscle as flab. Everyman as warrior. Every bank clerk, dermatologist or computer analyst who's ever had to back down from a fight in a bar, every little old lady who's been mugged in a supermarket parking lot, would identify with me. People would go to the fight for the same reason they go to the Indianapolis 500: to see someone get killed while hoping that he doesn't.

I'd not only make millions, I'd be worth it. Do you think the people who paid upwards of $1,500 to attend the fight feel ripped off? I'm talking about people like Madonna and Sean Penn, Malcolm Forbes, Jack Nicholson, Oprah Winfrey, Magic Johnson, Stephen King, Norman Mailer, Warren Beatty, Paul Simon. Not at all. They were there, they were seen, they exist. My contendership would serve the same function. It's not the content of the event that matters, it's the frame you put around it.

Remember this: HBO is broadcasting delayed telecasts of the fight next week. The delayed versions of the minute-and-a-half event will be one hour long. And they expect good ratings.

Tyson-Spinks may not have been a fight for the ages, but it certainly was a fight for this particular age.

Do you think the 1990s can be any worse? (1988)

True to the times, people are calling Tyson a great fighter and comparing him with Joe Louis, Rocky Marciano and Muhammad Ali. Give me a break.

Tyson is obviously a strong young man with a terrific punch, but he's twenty-one years old and has made his career punching out unemployed bartenders and overweight bouncers. Let him beat someone before we call him great. Failing that, let him at least beat a lot more nobodies. He has overcome great poverty to get where he is. To be really great, he shall have to overcome great wealth. His chances aren't that good.

Besides, I think the young Ali would have slapped him silly.

Sailing Along

I wish my father were alive to experience the Dennis Conner phenomenon—an international yachtsman becoming a national hero. I'd love to hear him laugh again. And I think I can imagine what he'd say, something like: "What's the matter? Has everybody gone crazy?"

We were a boating family. My father owned a boat, a kind of big rowboat with an outboard motor which we kept in our garage on a trailer. On the weekends we'd haul the thing over to the Detroit River and go fishing. That's what a boat was for, in my father's eyes, fishing.

Occasionally we'd troll out around Grosse Pointe, where the swells lived, and there would be the sailboats, insolently dotting the horizon.

"Gee, Dad," I remember saying, "sailing looks like fun."

"I suppose it is," he replied, "if you don't have anything better to do."

Well, now we have a man who has had hardly anything better to do his whole life. Legend has it that Conner, who returned to the United States this week bearing the famous America's Cup which he wrested from the Aussies, has spent 10,000 hours of his life steering twelve-meter boats (which, against all reason, are sixty-five feet long). In return, he has been given all that a grateful country can give: a meeting with the president, a ticker tape parade in New York and a Wheaties commercial. He is Mary Lou Retton with a sunburn. We are now supposed to want to be like him when we grow up.

I don't. I think going out for a sail once in a while is O.K., but it's nothing I'd want to spend 10,000 hours doing. It's boring. The America's Cup races were boring, if you want to know the truth. Two boats get out there, one of them is faster and it wins. Also, the participants look like poster boys for the Skin Cancer Foundation.

That's not the main reason I don't want to be like Dennis Conner, though. He has been quoted as saying, of his recruiting technique:

"If a crew member will put this (sailing) ahead of his religion, his family, his girlfriend, his home, his career, then I'll give him a tryout."

Dennis Conner is a nut, and that's why I don't want to be like him. What we're talking about here, after all, is sailing a boat. It's not war or literature or even making money. It's more like spending money. Conner spent $20 million winning back the Cup. There's got to be something better to do with twenty mill than make a sailboat go fast.

President Reagan, at a White House ceremony, said:

"I just have to believe that it says something about the competitiveness of American technology that, this time around, the United States entered perhaps the best designed and most technologically advanced twelve-meter yacht ever christened."

And it does. It says we've got bright people spending their time and energy making toy boats go fast instead of doing something useful. Our reading scores are down, Johnny can't multiply and we're turning out a nation of scientific illiterates, but not to worry: we're competitive in yacht racing.

And even that isn't forever. We won out over essentially European and Australian competition this year. Now the Japanese have bought a couple of boats and are studying the problem. You want odds on saying sayonara to the Cup by 1993?

Still, I'm glad Conner won it for the San Diego Yacht Club, rather than for the New York Yacht Club, which had held the memento for 132 years prior to losing it in 1984. I have a personal grudge against the New York Yacht Club.

It was about fifteen years ago that I was walking down West Forty-fourth Street in Manhattan and noticed this remarkable building across the street. It was a typical, narrow commercial building except that it had the back of a Spanish galleon for a second-story window. It was a huge bay window that looked as though Errol Flynn should be climbing a rope toward it with a sword in his teeth. It was the New York Yacht Club.

"I know the New York Yacht Club," I said to myself. "It is where the America's Cup is. I'm an American, I think I'll go over and take a look.

I got three steps past the front door. "Where do you think you're going, buddy?" a doorman asked.

"I thought I might take a look at America's Cup," I said. "I'm an American."

"Members only, buddy," the doorman replied. "Out." I had my best bowling jacket on too. The one that says "Lempke's Funeral Home" on the back.

I was glad when New York lost the Cup in 1984 and happy that it didn't win it back. The current winner, the San Diego Yacht Club, has promised to send the hardware on tour and perhaps put it on permanent display where real people can see it, rather than just yachtsmen.

If we're expected to be patriotic about something, we may as well know what it looks like. (1987)

Time Warp

As some of you might remember, I was for years Iowa's resident expert on six-girl basketball. Yes, many's the long evening I've spent watching young, feminine bodies crash to the floor in the name of athletic competition. They felt like long evenings, anyway.

I don't wish to brag but it was I who coined many of the terms by which the game is now defined. Traditional techniques such as the standing jump shot, the slow-break offense, the near-dribble and the medicine ball lob had no names until I came along. I was also the first to identify the classic defense of girls basketball: Standing in One Place and Waving Your Hands a Lot.

But I suppose my greatest contribution to the game was the discovery of its origins, which I happened upon while doing research at the British Museum in London.

It seems that in prehistoric times women of rival villages, as a break from cave work, would stand on either side of a line and throw rocks at each other. The men would stand on the side and laugh.

Through the centuries they kept reducing the number of players and rocks until they got to six players and one rock, later symbolized by a ball. That was the state of the game when it arrived by stage-coach in Iowa. It has remained little changed since.

Oh, I know, they let girls play boys' basketball these days as a concession to the twentieth century, but I find it an inferior game, almost without humor. Real girls' basketball is six-on-six or, rather, three-plus-three on three-plus-three. There's no other game like it.

I went to Veterans Memorial Auditorium to see Saturday's state tournament final between North Iowa, of Buffalo Center, and Atlantic, of Atlantic. I had not seen a game in years but I am happy to report that the sport has lost nothing of its charm. It still combines the action of shuffleboard with the tension of checkers and the grace of slam dancing.

But the Iowa tournament is more than just the games. It is a vehicle for community pride, a showcase for youthful ebullience and the occasion for pageantry that makes the Orange Bowl half-time show look like a Las Vegas saloon act.

At a time when college athletics look grubbier and grubbier (who cares whether your hired guns can beat our hired guns?) it is left to the high schools to epitomize the true values of sport—sacrifice, discipline, dedication and plain fun. The girls' state tournament does that about as well as it can be done.

The tournament won my heart permanently a number of years back when it turned down a chance to be on a national television show because the show's producers wanted the championship game staged at a different time—Sunday morning I think it was. No, said the Iowa people, we're a Saturday night event. And so they are.

It's a great show. Where else can you see a basketball player in full battle dress wearing a corsage? (1990)

This old homesick heart got quite a wrench the other day. A reader sent me a report on a recent girls' basketball game and suddenly I was back in Iowa, watching athletically clad, nubile maidens in kneepads pursue floor burns.

The game reported on was a classic, everything a girl's basketball game should be and less. Thrills, tension, drama, standing around; it had it all. It went into four overtime periods, and when it was over the undefeated Melvin team had trounced Sibley by the score of 4–2. The score at the end of regulation was 0–0.

Melvin's star, Deb Mouw, scored the winning basket. The story didn't say who scored the losing one, but that's the way journalism goes sometimes.

At first I thought that the baskets were late getting back from the cleaners and they'd started without them. Then I thought that maybe the referee had forgotten the ball. Or even, perhaps, that the girls had played the game under the impression that they were posing for their team pictures.

But no, none of that was true. What happened was that one of the coaches tried to slow down the game and stopped it altogether, by accident. Then they couldn't get it started again.

That doesn't mean it wasn't a tough game, of course. There were a number of casualties. Two girls caught cold. A referee's foot fell asleep. A radio announcer suffered an attack of lockjaw in the opening minutes and nobody noticed until the third overtime.

The real girls' basketball fans in the crowd didn't complain, though. They knew what they had come to see and they were seeing it—boredom under pressure.

A lot of people say that the girls should copy the professionals and adopt a twenty-four-second clock. I'm against it; it would ruin the essential rhythms of the game.

They should use an hour glass. (1979)

Grandma's Moment of Truth

I am not one of those fanatics who think hunters should be shot. While I am not a hunter myself, I see nothing irredeemably corrupt in the practice of going into the fields and blowing Walt Disney creatures to bits. A little depraved, perhaps, but not irredeemably corrupt.

I eat meat and I realize that it isn't created in a cellophane wrap, suitable for freezing, in a supermarket. It was once an animal that had to be killed, and I accept responsibility. I do not feel morally superior to those who prefer to go out and kill the poor little beasts themselves.

What I object to are hunters who make a big thing out of it. You know, people like Hemingway, who made this noble ritual out of the practice of shooting things with fur on them, as though it were a difficult or even courageous thing to do.

I ran across the tracks of such a hunter just the other day. He's Ron Schara, an outdoors writer for the *Minneapolis Tribune.* I don't know the gentleman, but he suffers from one of the worst cases of galloping Hemingwayitis I've ever seen. Here is how he began a recent column:

"There are moments of truth unknown except to those who hunt and fish.

"The sudden flurry of a hooked steelhead is a gut-wrenching, draining experience . . . [And that's only what it's like for the fisherman; imagine what it must be like for the fish.]

"But no moment compares with the final act of a hunt for white-tailed bucks. It stands alone because the white-tailed deer stands alone and supreme in the forest . . ." [Or as alone and supreme as you can stand surrounded by red-faced men equipped with high-powered rifles.]

Schara goes on to talk about the "moment of truth" that plagues "every sensitive deer hunter." One is tempted to say, "Both of them?" —but one won't say it. Let Schara continue.

"The moment is that time when the deer is first heard and then seen.

"The moment is when your breath is short and your tongue is thicker than your dry mouth.

"The moment is that instant when the wind's direction, a trivial item in most lives, becomes a dominating force.

"The moment is when the click of the gun safety, the swish of a coat, the scrape of tree bark sound louder than hail on a tin roof.

"The moment is when you are alone with the white-tail."

Don't be afraid, Schara; it's not going to bite you. It's not as though you were stalking something dangerous, like a rat in an alley, for example.

I don't mean to be too hard on Mr. Schara. My paternal grandmother shared his enthusiasm for killing game animals. It was my

Ukrainian grandmother. The basic difference between her and Schara is that, instead of killing deer, she killed chickens.

She would go to the market and buy a live chicken and bring it home in a sack. She would carry the chicken by the legs into the back yard, where she had a little stool set up by a stump.

This, I suppose, was her moment of truth. She'd be alone in the back yard, just her and the chicken.

Carefully, with elegant grace, she would grasp the chicken in her two hands and wring its neck. The sound was louder than hail on a roof. (I don't know whether her tongue became thicker than her dry mouth at this point—I never thought to ask—but I wouldn't be surprised.)

Having wrung the chicken's neck, she would lay the bird on the stump and sever its head from its body in one clean, precise stroke of her hatchet. (Oh, didn't I tell you about her hatchet? She had one.) Then she would release the body of the chicken to flutter around the yard for a while. The ritual over, she would plunge the chicken into a pot of water she had boiled for the occasion, then pluck the chicken. I don't mean to boast about a relative, but my grandmother could really pluck a chicken. Hemingway himself could not have done it any better.

She was a hell of a sportswoman.

The odd thing is, she never bragged about it. She never spoke of her courage, even though it is probably more dangerous to kill a chicken with one's bare hands than it is to kill a deer with a rifle.

It was simply something she did. Great white hunters like Schara could take a lesson from her. (1981)

8

FOOLS, CHARLATANS, SCOUNDRELS AND THE OTHER RECOGNIZED PROFESSIONS

I AM FORCED by greed from time to time to give speeches. Mainly I give them to professional groups and mainly I attack the group I'm speaking to. (As the scorpion said, it's my nature.)

Teachers are by far the best audience for this sort of thing. They nod in agreement as you catalogue their failings and come up to you after the speech to confess their guilt. It comes from not making a lot of money.

Lawyers are easily the most cheerful audience. Assault them savagely, give them the worst you have about their profession; they merely laugh and hoot, then top your lawyer stories with examples of their own. It comes from making a lot of money.

Doctors, on the other hand, are a different breed. I once told a group of physicians that, with the possible exception of the Mafia, the medical profession was more responsible for the drug culture of this nation than any other group. I then made the tactical error of asking for questions.

It is a measure of how inferior the liberal arts education we give our doctors is that some of them think "You cretin!" is a question. When you insult doctors, they get insulted. It comes from being God.

House Calls and Other Folk Medicine

The head of University Hospitals says he is "uncomfortable" with the new law that allows indigent women to deliver their babies at hospitals near their home towns rather than traveling to his facility in Iowa City. The law, he says, will reduce the number of births at the hospital to the bare minimum needed for the purposes of medical instruction.

"A lot of people view this problem from the service dimension only, but there's also the question of the educational function," the gentleman, John Colloton, says.

Well, sure. Of course. How can we expect our sons and daughters to become competent physicians unless we give them poor people to practice on? My God, if they run out of indigents at University Hospitals, the next thing you know they'll be forced to turn the students loose on real people. You and me, even.

I'm not sure I agree entirely with Mr. Colloton's solution to the problem, however. Poor folk, as we know, are a hardy lot without the tender sensibilities characteristic of those of us with money, but is it really fair to make those pregnant women schlep all the way across the state to have their babies, away from the emotional support of friends and family? Damn me for a liberal if you will, but it doesn't seem right.

I would prefer a solution more in keeping with the times. If we need more poor people, let's create them.

I would have thought the Reagan administration was doing a pretty good job of that already, but if there aren't enough poor people to go around we can always redouble our efforts. We can cut our educational budgets (except for the money that goes to football and basketball, of course). We can lower the minimum wage. We can make the lottery compulsory. Why, before you knew it, the young doctors at Iowa City would be groaning under their caseloads.

There is another solution available, but I hesitate to mention it, it's so silly. If I tell you, you have to promise not to laugh. OK, here it is:

The doctors could go to the patients.

You're laughing and you promised not to. I know, there is no one to teach them how. Hardly a living doctor has ever made a house call. But I'm sure they could find some old, retired codger who could teach one class at the med school—Home Delivery of Services 101. I'd love to sit in on the first class. Picture the scene.

The old doctor appears before the class and sets up an easel with a picture of a house on it. He motions to it with a pointer. "This is a picture of a house," he says.

"Why is it so small?" one of the brighter students asks.

"Because it is the house of a patient. They tend to be smaller than the houses of doctors."

"Why?"

"Because there is more money in treating an illness than in having one," the doctor says.

"Gee, doctor, this is interesting," another student says.

"Now, when making a house call, you get into your car with a small black bag of instruments and go to the patient's house. Any questions so far?"

"Yes, sir, is this patient a friend of yours?"

"Not necessarily."

"Then why would you want to go into the house?"

"The patient might be too sick to go out."

"Isn't that why they make ambulances?"

"Yes, but that's another course, Collecting Patients 407."

"Isn't that taught in the business school?"

"No, that's Collecting From Patients 707. Gentlemen! You two in the back there. Stop fighting. What do you think you're doing?"

"Jeffrey took my stethoscope and went 'Bleah!' real loud into it. He almost blew out my eardrums. So I hit him."

"How many times must I tell you, the stethoscope should be worn around the neck while not in use, not in the ears. Any more such outbreaks and I shall have you transferred to the nursing school. Where was I?"

"You were making social calls on sick people you didn't know."

"No, no, you don't understand. This isn't about social calls. You make house calls to treat the patient or to diagnose his illness to find out whether he needs more sophisticated treatment."

"How can you diagnose his illness if you can't hook him up to the hospital's expensive machines?"

You can't, always, but you can do a pretty decent preliminary job with the tools in your little black bag."

"That's not what they told us in Making the Most of Your Professional Opportunities 301."

"I don't think they had that course when I went to school. I'm afraid I'm a little behind the times."

"So is this course, professor. So is this course."

I told you it was silly. Scratch the house calls idea. Better to go on creating poor people. It's more practical. (1986)

The American Nurses Association voted not to take part in civil-defense plans.

"Since nurses are involved in protecting and preserving health," its resolution said, "by making plans on coping with the aftermath of a nuclear war, they might mislead people into thinking that nuclear war is survivable."

Now that makes sense to me. Why doesn't the American Medical Association, the doctors' union, make a statement like that? Aren't they supposed to be smarter than nurses?

I suppose the question answers itself.

A Cure for Lawyers

We have a new crisis. Add it to the budget crisis, the crisis in education, the AIDS crisis and the crisis in Central America. It is the liability insurance crisis.

Liability insurance, according to current hysteria, is out of control. Damage claims are skyrocketing, as are insurance rates. Insurance companies are dropping certain kinds of coverage and many doctors, particularly obstetricians, are giving up their professions to become garage mechanics. Things are that bad.

Politicians are falling over themselves in an effort to make things better. Some states have put caps on certain kinds of damage awards and a presidential commission has recommended restricting punitive damages and awards for "pain and suffering," as well as putting a limit on attorneys' fees.

How ingenious. How complex. How dumb.

It is as though a province in India noticed that an unusually high percentage of its citizens was being eaten by tigers and decided to deal with the problem by putting a quota on the number of citizens each tiger could eat. Or making it illegal to allow one's self to be eaten by a tiger.

Provinces in India don't do that. When they experience a tiger crisis they go right to the heart of the problem, which is a surplus of tigers. They stage a tiger hunt.

In somewhat the same way, the root cause of our liability crisis is that we have too many lawyers. Possibly you've heard the story about the fellow who opened a law office in a town that had no lawyers and found he wasn't making a living? Until a second lawyer started a practice across the street, and there was more than enough business for both of them. That is the nature of lawyers; the more of them there are, the merrier they get.

You think that's an exaggeration, don't you? Let me give you an example: About a year ago a fellow in Washington, D.C., bought a used BMW sedan from a dealer for $19,600. Shortly thereafter the FBI showed up at his house and confiscated the car. It had been stolen. The man sued the dealer and was awarded $28,000, which covered his loss, the cost of renting a substitute car and . . . his lawyer's fee. The dealer then sued the man who sold him the car and got $33,000, the twenty-eight grand . . . plus attorneys' fees. That man has sued the man who sold *him* the car who has sued a dealer who sold him the car who was planning on suing the rent-a-car company from which he bought the car. At each point, a lawyer will rake in a bit of the pot. Before it is over, that BMW will be a $60,000 car: $20,000 in transportation and $40,000 in lawyers. Is that any way to run a country?

Japan certainly isn't run that way. In Japan they don't encourage their best and brightest to enter a profession that divides up pies rather than bakes them, that makes money rather than creates wealth. Japan, by the way, does not have a liability insurance crisis.

We have to get rid of some of our lawyers. I don't suggest staging a lawyer hunt, except perhaps as a last resort, but there are some intermediate measures that might be taken:

• **Close all law schools at publicly supported universities.** I've already suggested Iowa should do this with the school at Iowa City, but it should be a nationwide movement. There is no good reason for tax money being used for the training of people who, for the most part, will spend their lives helping people and corporations escape justice and evade taxes. What little legitimate call there is for that sort of thing can be answered by private schools. If we found ourselves running short of prosecutors, we might follow the example of West Point and Annapolis and open up a few "legal service academies" at public schools for the express purpose of training prosecutors and give the students a free education in return for a commitment to work for a time putting bad guys in jail.

• **Make ethics mandatory.** Fully a third of the profession could be eliminated if you pulled the licenses of lawyers who failed to live up to even a rudimentary definition of honesty and fair play.

• **Put the United States Attorney General's office under the Department of Agriculture.** If the USDA could do for lawyers what it's done for farmers, our surplus lawyer problem would be over within the decade.

Perhaps you think you detect a flaw in this plan. Wouldn't it create a shortage of lawyers, you ask, which would have the effect of jacking up legal prices?

No, it wouldn't. There is no such thing as a shortage of lawyers. Remember the rule: The more lawyers, the more for them to do; fewer lawyers, less work.

The legal profession doesn't respond to the laws of supply and demand. With lawyers, supply *is* demand. (1986)

Reverse Discrimination

I ran across a poignant story in the *New York Times* the other day, an age-old story of white men and Indians, of promises unkept and treaties broken, of land stolen.

You really have to watch those Indians.

What happened was that in 1959 the White Mountain Apaches began leasing home sites to white-eyes at their Fort Apache Indian Reservation in Arizona.

It soon became an idyllic resort community, centered around man-made, trout-stocked Hawley Lake. More and more non-Indians came, first building humble cabins, then adding on until they had luxury dwellings, worth as much as $200,000.

The leases were dirt cheap, $40 to $130 a year, but they were for only twenty-five years. That didn't worry the white settlers, though.

"At the time of the leases, we were told that they would be renewed at the end of the twenty-five years, nothing to worry about," says the president of the Hawley Lake Homeowners Association.

Well, you know what they say about an oral promise: It's not worth the smoke signal it's written with. In any case, the Indians now don't want to renew the leases. As the leases run out, they want the white-eyes to vacate the property. They can take their homes with them if they want, so long as they go.

"We all feel that we're getting a real raw deal out of it," the association's president says.

"They've got no beef coming," answers the Apache tribal chairman. "They lived up there for nothing for twenty-five years. To me, that's a lifetime."

The Apaches haven't decided what they're going to do with the land, yet. They may attempt a big resort development or just let it revert to its natural state.

"Just to have that land and walk in the quiet pine trees with nobody around is a priceless, million-dollar feeling to an Apache," the tribe's leader says.

I called a land developer friend of mine in the area, Chauncey Sweetbreath, to find out the real story.

"It's an outrage," he said. "Another example of fast-talking Indians taking advantage of the innocence of suburbanites of primitive intelligence."

"You think the Indians cheated the white guys, then?" I asked.

"Of course they did. They probably poured out a pitcher or two of martinis when it came time to sign the leases. You know how middle-class Americans are. Give them a few martinis and they'll sign anything. They can't hold their liquor."

"I always thought it was Native Americans who couldn't hold their liquor."

"Sure, that's what they want you to believe. But remember that time they got a bunch of Dutch settlers drunk and palmed off Manhattan on them in exchange for $25 worth of beads? I'll bet those beads are worth thousands of dollars by now and Manhattan is an open sewer. I'm telling you, those Indians are shrewd."

"Why do you think the Apaches won't renew the leases at Hawley Lake?"

"I hate to make charges I can't prove, but I honestly think it's genocide."

"You can't be serious!"

"I'm afraid I am. The American Indian is engaged in a long-term conspiracy to do away with the white man by forcing him into crowded cities with bad air and a high crime rate."

"Why, that's diabolical."

"Yeah, the Indian line is that non-Indians prefer to live in urban squalor, but that's racist nonsense."

"I should say so."

"The truth is, they give us little choice. They've taken all of the choice desert locations. My grandfather helped settle Hawley Lake in 1959. He was the first one in the community to have a golf cart. I have roots there and it's a bitter thing to think of it reverting to nature."

"I can imagine."

"But there's nothing we can do about it, I guess. We'll just have to learn from experience. You know what they say: 'Indian fool white man once, shame on Indian; Indian fool white man twice, shame on white man.'" And, with those words, he hung up. I hadn't heard such a sad story since that time Poland invaded Germany. (1984)

Do-Gooders

A federal judge has awarded Jim Bakker, television's answer to Elmer Gantry, an expense-paid vacation for the next forty-five years in recognition of his work in swindling the terminally naive. Of course, Bakker has to live in and his wife can only visit him on weekends but, as he well knows, expense-paid vacations don't come cheap. I thought the sentence astonishing.

We are not accustomed to seeing our white collar criminals treated so harshly. Let a man fleece society of millions and a judge is apt to give him a stern talking to and sentence him to six months of community service at a singles bar. Serial killers don't get forty-five years in jail. That's a tough judge.

How tough? When Bakker's nineteen-year-old daughter, Tammy Sue, burst into disconsolate sobs at hearing the sentence, the judge, Robert Potter, snarled, "Any more outbursts and I'll have the marshals get you out."

Too tough, I think. I'm all for throwing the book at white collar criminals and the Reverend Bakker was a particularly cheesy example of the breed, but it's not as though he didn't give *any* value for the money he skimmed. For months on end he and his remarkable wife, Tammy Fay, have regaled us with a story of sin, sex and salvation, not to mention wretched excess, that not even daytime television could match. I thought it especially droll when he hid under his lawyer's couch during the trial, claiming to be cleft from reason. I think the judge should have given Bakker some credit for that.

Jimbo's real crime, I suppose, lay in being a religious crook. Had he been your average, run-of-the-mill hustler he could have claimed to have found God while awaiting trial and thrown himself on the mercy of the court, as is the fashion.

But he had already found God. He was the mirror image of Mark Twain's old lady, the one who didn't drink or smoke. When she fell ill she had nothing to give up. "She had neglected her vices," Twain said.

Bakker's problem was precisely the reverse: he had assumed all the virtues *before* his fall. When his moment of judgment came, he had no fresh ones in which to cloak himself.

Not so with Zsa Zsa Gabor who, if she were not of easy virtue, would be of no virtue at all. Cruel coincidence bracketed her sentence for slugging a police officer with Bakker's send-off, diminishing it. She got three days in jail, 120 hours of community service and a fine amounting to $12,350. She got off cheap. When I was a kid growing up on the near-northwest side of Detroit, slugging a cop was considered a very serious offense. You were lucky if the case got to a judge. More often the cop sentenced you to 120 hours in the emergency room of the nearest hospital and you walked with a limp for a long time after.

I've never understood the Zsa Zsa phenomenon. Television has accustomed us to people of no discernible talent becoming famous, but not to staying famous for forty years as Ms. Gabor has. Her undiscernible talents must be amazing. I always thought the best characterization of her was delivered by that malicious wit, Oscar Levant, who called her "a social worker for the rich."

And, speaking of the rich, the untalented and the fake, Ronald and Nancy Reagan made their triumphal tour of Japan this week. Some observers were amazed at the outpouring of warmth and affection for Mr. Reagan, who is said to be getting $2 million for troubling to make the trip. I was not.

The Japanese have just lost a beloved emperor who lived forever, didn't do much and denied knowledge of all the bad things that happened during his reign. The Japanese think Ronald Reagan is Hirohito's clone.

I do think Mrs. Reagan is getting a bad rap on her forthcoming book, however. She is being criticized in some quarters for writing a mean-spirited and self-serving account of events while she was first lady. If you can't be mean-spirited and self-serving when writing your memoirs, what's the sense of writing them?

I also think she's been unfairly ridiculed for her involvement with astrology. She is said to have spent $3,000 a month on astrological advice, which she would then pass on to her husband to guide his career.

It was money well-spent, as far as I'm concerned. Mr. Reagan's success in everything he's ever put his hand to cannot be accounted for by other than supernatural means. Astrology's as good an explanation as any. (1989)

The Reverend Mr. Bakker's sentence was later overturned by an appeals court.

A Liberal's Conservative

I have a dream. I am a United States senator on the judiciary committee. Before me is Supreme Court nominee Robert Bork. My turn to question him arrives.

"Judge Bork," I say, "is it true that on at least seven occasions since you became a federal judge, you have committed acts of certiorari with consenting adults?"

A look of horror freezes on Bork's face. His rheumy eyes begin to water. "I don't know," he says. "That is to say, I'm not sure of the number. Seven times was it? Do you have a page number on that?"

I press on. "And isn't it also true that, as a result of this behavior, you have contracted a severe case of stare decisis, and are under treatment for it even now?"

"I wouldn't call it treatment, Senator," he says. "It's more like a salve."

"And further," I say, by this time crawling onto the top of my desk on all fours, "in the famous case of Snopes vs. Backwater, Mississippi, didn't you rule that a meter maid could force a motorist to shove beans up his nose if she found him double-parked?"

"Yes, that was the result of the decision, but I was unable to find anything in the Constitution protecting people from beans in their noses."

"And in the even more famous case of Dipstick vs. All the Bad People in Texas," I say, now standing on top of my desk, "didn't you rule that deputy county sheriffs could force unborn pregnant mothers to do the Hokeypokey without regard to their personal safety?"

"Yes, I did, but I was under the impression that case fell under the Fifth Commandment, rather than the Fifth Amendment. I made a mistake; I admit it."

"I put it to you that it was not a mistake but instead a consistent pattern of favoring unfettered monopolistic power of multi-lateral corporations, Gestapo police tactics and dirty dancing. I further put it to you that you have a long personal history of running amber lights, not returning library books on time and tearing the tags off mattresses. Can you tell us why this committee should not reject your nomination to the highest court in the land and rescind your driver's license?"

At this Bork bursts into tears and says: "You're right, senator, I'm unworthy. I don't know what ever made me think I was fit to serve on the Supreme Court. I withdraw my nomination, and I intend to enter a monastery the first thing Monday."

I climb off my desk to the wild applause of the audience, including television technicians.

Too bad life isn't like that. Certainly the Bork hearings weren't. They were much less exciting, one might even say dull.

Which is okay; there's no particular reason for confirmation hearings to rival "Miami Vice" as melodrama. But I didn't think Judge Bork lived up to his billing. He was supposed to be this witty, warm, right-wing intellectual who would wow us with his incandescent arguments.

He didn't. What he did instead is retreat from his earlier stated positions until he was all but indistinguishable from a moderate liberal trying to get on the court. On issue after issue he said that he had changed his mind or that he felt a precedent had been set which he would not overturn.

To tell you the truth, he didn't look so good. You had to wonder, as several senators did out loud, which Bork was going to wind up on the Supreme Court, the flamboyant conservative who speaks with high disdain of the work of recent courts, or the mild-mannered rationalist who would go along with the crowd. That tape that Ted Kennedy played, the one in which Bork is telling law students that precedent doesn't mean much in constitutional cases, is so at variance with what he's telling the committee now that you have to doubt his sincerity.

I know one thing, though: I'd vote for him in a minute.

I say that even though, from a liberal point of view, I agree he will be a terrible judge, and that's true no matter which Bork we get. Giving him the best of it, he has a very narrow view of the Constitution's ability to protect individuals from the tyranny of the state. He has, however, three things going for him:

- He is sixty years old.
- He is a chain smoker.
- He drinks some; maybe more than some.

In short, he does not look like a man who is going to be on the court twenty years or so. He probably won't last ten.

The alternative Reagan nominee is likely to be just as conservative as Bork, be not as smart and have a clean liver. You put him on the court and he's there until 2015, doing mischief.

I think Robert Bork is the best offer the liberals are going to get from President Reagan. They should snap him up. (1987)

Mr. Justice Peepers

The big question posed by the nomination of David Souter to the Supreme Court is obvious:

Do we want a Supreme Court justice who looks as though his mother dresses him?

After listening to him testify for three days before the Senate Judiciary Committee, the answer is pretty clear: Why not? Put a robe on him and no one will know the difference.

The second big question about Souter was how he felt about abortion rights.

At this point, nobody knows. Or if they know, they're not telling; certainly Souter isn't.

The senators on the committee tried to poke around in Judge Souter's psyche to find out how he felt about Roe vs. Wade, the 1973 Supreme Court decision that made abortion legal, but he wasn't having any.

"I have not got any agenda on what should be done with Roe vs. Wade if that case were brought before me," he said.

"I will listen to both sides of that case. I have not made up my mind. And I do not go on the court saying I must go one way or I must go another way."

He lied, of course. *Everybody* has an agenda on Roe vs. Wade, even people who haven't heard of it. If you think about anything at all, you think from time to time on the awesome dilemma facing a woman who, blameless or not, faces an unwanted pregnancy. That's Roe vs. Wade.

One would have to assume that Judge Souter is anti-abortion rights. One of his main sponsors in getting this nomination was George Bush's chief of staff, John Sununu, a fellow New Hampshireperson. They've known each other for years. Why would Sununu plug someone for the job if he wasn't sure the person was going to vote Bush's way on abortion?

On the other hand, maybe Judge Souter didn't lie to the committee, maybe he lied to the White House.

Either way, I wouldn't blame him. Everybody lies a little bit when interviewing for a job. There's plenty of time for truth when you retire.

Senator Howard Metzenbaum of Ohio attempted to find out how Judge Souter felt about the anguish of a woman facing an unwanted pregnancy. Souter responded with a story about a pregnant girl he once counseled while he was a dormitory adviser at Harvard. The point of the story was that he knew about unwanted pregnancy because he'd met someone who had one once.

The committee members bought it. That's the other thing that's become clear during these hearings: You don't have to be real smart to be a United States senator. They sit there and read questions staff members have prepared for them:

"How do you feel about the use of original dictum in the famous case of Slime vs. the Congenitally Bewildered of Indiana?"

And Souter, no dummy he, will say: "An interesting case in that it confronts the problem of congenital certiorari with a slight excursion into ex deus rectum, to say nothing of sic semper tyrannis."

He will go on like that for a while until he pauses long enough for the committee to be sure he's finished, upon which the senator who asked the question will nod thoughtfully and say: "I'm not sure I don't agree with you." He is also not sure what the question was, let alone the answer. It's all fairly amusing in a boring way.

By the end of his testimony Souter had made himself so acceptable to the moderates on the committee that the conservatives were beginning to get upset. They thought he was sounding like something left over from the Carter administration.

Particularly unsettling to them was Judge Souter's stated willingness to have the Supreme Court fill vacuums created by Congress's inaction in dealing with pressing social problems. Senator Arlen Spector of Pennsylvania, with perhaps more candor than he intended, said:

"If Congress decides to sit passively, the Congress is deciding not to act. Perhaps our strongest ability is to do nothing." It's not often you hear a senator blurt out the truth like that.

The odds-on betting is that Judge Souter will be confirmed. I am ambivalent about the prospect.

On the one hand, I rather like the idea of having a gnostic on the court, a man who does not read newspapers, watch television or listen to the radio, whose idea of a zippy time is cracking walnuts.

On the other hand, anyone who gets the highest rating of the American Bar Association can't be all good. (1990)

The First Recorded Confirmation Hearing

Attila: Mr. Chairman, ladies and gentlemen, fellow Huns; I am very pleased to appear before this distinguished committee today to have my qualifications reviewed. I am honored to have been chosen Scourge of God-Designate and promise you that, if confirmed, I shall do my utmost to see to it that Europe trembles at my very name.

We face a critical time in the life of our nation. The threat of Christianity grows daily, and a serious looting and pillaging gap has opened up between us and the Vandals. There are those who say that our best rapine days are behind us. I don't agree with that. There is no reason that we can't get this country moving again—if we have but the will. Give me a few thousand good men and horses and I will make the Visigoths look like a punk-rock group. I am prepared to answer any questions you might have.

Chairman: Thank you very much, Mr. Hun. The committee appreciates your forthrightness and frankness. I would like to say for the record that I've known the nominee and his brother, Bleda, since they were little boys setting fire to tents, and I've never known a finer scourge. His career stands as a shining beacon of unconscionable behavior in a sea of weakness. I for one am proud to have such a fine young man nominated to such an important position, and I look forward to voting for his confirmation. And now, questions from the other members of the committee.

Senator Larry: Mr. Hun, the chairman mentioned your brother, Bleda. Isn't it true that you recently had him murdered?

Attila: I was hoping we could get through these hearings without dragging personalities into it but, since you mention Bleda, I confess that I did indeed have him put to death. He was always a snotty kid. I suppose that, with the benefit of twenty-twenty hindsight, I could have taken some other course of action—I could have had his tongue torn out, for example—but I don't see what's to be gained by raking over the coals of a two-bit fratricide. You can't second-guess yourself.

Senator Mo: What is your philosophical approach to looting and pillaging?

Attila: Balance. A strong National Offense Posture demands both a pillaging and looting capability. I think you have to avoid extremists on both sides of the question.

Senator Curley: Are you suggesting, then, that there is no place in modern warfare for rape?

Attila: Not at all. I would hate to see a time when the sacking of cities was not attended by the screams of women. I was simply being responsive to the senator's question.

Senator Curley: Speaking of the sacking of cities, should you be confirmed as Scourge of God—and I have no reason to doubt that you will be—what would be your policy toward Rome?

Attila: I have not yet had the opportunity to study that issue as carefully as I would wish but, speaking generally, I think I can promise that, if confirmed, my policy toward Rome would be . . . toward Rome.

Senator Mo: In case of an armed conflict, would you be willing to use the long bow?

Attila: Senator, I think that to unilaterally renounce the use of any weapon, no matter how terrible, is to encourage aggression. A city worth plundering is worth fighting for.

Chairman: Let me interject here that it is refreshing to hear before this committee a young man to whom plunder is not a dirty word. The policy of appeasement followed by his predecessors has brought us to the brink of being liked by our neighbors. I look forward to a time when Mr. Hun can restore our national honor.

Attila: I thank the chair and assure him that I will do everything in my power to see to it that his confidence in me is not misplaced. If I could sum up my philosophy of life in a single phrase, it would be "No more Mr. Nice Guy."

Senator Larry: Mr. Hun, to avoid even the appearance of a potential conflict of interests, are you willing to put all your assets in a blind trust?

Attila: I certainly am, Senator. In anticipation of my confirmation, I have already poked out the eyes of a trusted Venetian aide.

Senator Larry: That should do it, then. Good Luck, Mr. Hun. I think you're going to be one hell of a scourge. (1981)

By the way, if there's anyone out there I haven't insulted, please send me a self-addressed, stamped envelope, and I'll mail you a personal affront. Don't thank me; I am a full-service smart aleck.

9

THE EVIL THAT MEN DO

*D*AMN ME FOR *a woolly-headed liberal, but I happen to be one of those poor unfortunates who think that guns kill people. They're not the only things that kill people—there's Congress, for example—but they're certainly one of them. If they didn't kill people, why would they give them to soldiers?*

Do not be alarmed, however; I can do no harm. The clear-thinking intellectuals who make up the National Rifle Association are far more influential than I. They have bamboozled a large share of elected officials into believing that they represent the gun owners of America when, as any fool can tell, they are nothing more than a gun sellers' lobby. They would put nuclear weapons under the protection of the Second Amendment if they could get away with it (and with the way things are going, they may yet).

They will see to it that you will never want for a gun to pick up and shoot, whatever the reason.

And yet the NRA is not the source of our troubles, merely a symbol of them. Read these and weep:

Shooting Pains

I'm beginning to feel almost sorry for the people over at the National Rifle Association headquarters. Every time they get their public relations machine cranked up to tell us what a terrible thing a ban on semi-automatic weapons would be, how it would rape the Constitution and end freedom in these United States as we know it, some cuckoo sprays a bunch of innocent people with bullets, putting holes in their argument, to say nothing of the people.

141

The NRA people are then forced to claim that the gun had nothing to do with the incident, that the kook could have done as much damage with a knife or sharp popsicle stick. And they have to do it with straight faces!

I suppose we're in for a good dose of that guns-don't-kill-people baloney now, since that fellow in Louisville mowed down a crowd with his little semi-automatic the other day. "He should have been in jail; he should have been in a loony bin; he should have been put to sleep," the NRA apologists will be saying. It can't be easy, being a professional gun nut; you look foolish so much of the time.

I really think that a good many of the NRA types are buckling under the absurdity of their position; they're beginning to go bonkers. Did you see what Harlon Carter, the organization's executive vice-president, suggested as a proper way to fight the war on drugs?

"The emergency powers of the presidency should be invoked," he wrote in the NRA magazine. "Let us suspend the privilege of the writ of habeas corpus . . . drug dealers, distributors, transporters, possessors and users of drugs unlawfully obtained would be arrested without warrant and taken promptly before a federal committing officer . . ." who would send them to "a place prepared for internment for the duration of the war on drugs."

He suggests that the "internment facilities" be located in the desert regions of the southwest, at least thirty miles from human habitation. They would be surrounded by concentric rings of fences and barbed wire, patrolled by Doberman pinchers. No air conditioning. No television. No radio. You can tell this guy is really getting off on this. He says:

"No access would be permitted attorneys, congressmen or sob-sisters, super-saturated with sympathy for somebody—anybody—except at such time in the future as the victorious end of the war would permit hearings. Press and television would absolutely be denied access and in no event would they be permitted closer than thirty miles of the nearest human habitation." Unidentified aircraft flying near would be shot down.

The next thing, he'll be telling us that the CIA is controlling his mind with a transmitter implanted in a wisdom tooth. And the NRA isn't the only gun organization out there, or even the nuttiest. I keep getting mail from the "Citizens Committee for the Right to Keep and Bear Arms." It is apparently for people not smart enough to pass the NRA entrance exam. Dan Quayle is on their national advisory council.

Their latest letter, from the committee chairman to me, began: "Dear Trusted Friend." Right away you know he's not playing with a full deck. He goes on to express fear that supporters of the CCRKBA aren't getting all the mail that the committee is sending out. He'd heard that as much as 16 percent of all "nonprofit" rate mail was never delivered, so he asks his trusted friends to send back an acknowledgment of this last letter and with it, just to make sure the stamp doesn't go to waste, a donation. The donation will be used to bludgeon more spineless politicians over the head with bang-bang propaganda.

I didn't answer the letter. Let him think it got lost in the mail.

Actually, I'm no great believer in gun control anymore. The NRA has done its work too well; there are too many guns out there for a few more or a few less to make a difference. I simply hate to see the American people taken for fools by a lobby whose main interest is making money for gun manufacturers and sellers.

The *New York Times* recently recounted the tragic story of Karen Ann Wood, a young Maine mother of infant twin daughters, who was shot to death last year in the backyard of her suburban home when she went outdoors wearing white mittens and was apparently mistaken for a deer. A Maine grand jury failed to indict her killer for manslaughter. The intimation was that she was at fault for wearing the white mittens outside during hunting season.

See there? Guns don't kill people; mittens do. (1989)

Ms. Wood's killer was later brought to trial and a jury of his peers acquitted him. Now we know why Maine doesn't have many people.

More Guns, More

Last week I went a little funny in the head and said some nasty things about the National Rifle Association. I called it a gun sellers' lobby and even suggested that we take political retribution against its friends. I don't know what could have come over me; I don't take drugs and I'm very careful about walking around in the sun without a hat. I apologize.

The truth is that the NRA is as fine a group of selfless, public-spirited citizens as walk our earth. Its only goal is to keep us safe from our enemies, including ourselves.

That insight arrived like a poke with a sharp stick when I read about the NRA's latest project: the repeal of the ban on the sale of new machine guns.

You see, last spring the miserable, Commie-loving wimps who make up the anti-gun lobby attached an amendment to an otherwise responsible (weak) gun law, prohibiting the sale of machine guns not already registered with the Bureau of Alcohol, Tobacco and Firearms. This, in effect, froze the number of machine guns legally in private hands at about 127,000.

Well, you can see the problem. What about the millions of law-abiding, God-fearing, brush-their-teeth-after-every-meal Americans who want a machine gun of their very own? The collectors. The duck hunters with bad eyes. They can't buy one without taking it away from another such American. It is grossly unfair and dangerous and vaguely unconstitutional.

Criminals will always be able to get machine guns, after all. How are decent citizens to defend themselves? Suppose thirty or forty muggers stepped out of an alley in front of you and all you had to fight them off with was a .45 caliber revolver and an umbrella? That's a terrifying prospect.

Never fear, the NRA is near. It is putting its full and considerable weight behind repeal of the ban. "It is our position that legally registered machine guns are not a crime problem," an NRA spokesperson said. Or, to put it another way:

MACHINE GUNS DON'T KILL PEOPLE QUICKLY,
IMPATIENT PEOPLE KILL PEOPLE QUICKLY.

Not everybody agrees. "The law enforcement community is going to resist repeal of this provision with all the force it can muster," said a spokesperson for the International Association of Chiefs of Police.

But the NRA didn't get where it is by letting a bunch of namby-pamby police chiefs tell it what to do. It will yank the leashes of its Congressional lap dogs and get its way; it always does. And this is only the beginning, folks. There are plenty more weapons that need to be made legal. In the years ahead we can look forward to defending ourselves with bazookas, hand grenades, land mines and rocket launchers, all legally. You will be able to cower in your home secure in the knowledge that if they come to get you, you can take one with you. Maybe two.

Thanks NRA. We needed that.

But enough of guns; let's talk of knives.

Last week, California Angel first baseman Wally Joyner was struck with a knife thrown from the stands at Yankee Stadium. It didn't cut him. He felt something brush against his arm and he looked down to see a knife with a five-inch blade lying on the grass.

Now, a lot of people are going to say they shouldn't allow knives in Yankee Stadium. Probably the same people who want to limit the sale of machine guns. The thing they forget is:

KNIVES DON'T KILL PEOPLE;
UNLESS YOU THROW THEM REAL GOOD.

The way to solve the problem is to have sharpshooters with telescopic sights stationed out there behind the center field scoreboard, and every time they see someone in the crowd pull out a knife, pick him off. Or her. That's the constitutional way of handling the problem, so you're not interfering with anyone's right to bear arms.

Or you could start arming baseball players so that they can defend themselves against their fans. I'll have to wait until the NRA puts out a position paper on the subject before I come to a final conclusion.

But enough of knives, let us talk of cars.

President Reagan has come out for allowing states to raise the fifty-five-mile-an-hour speed limit on certain roads if they wish to. Finally an issue on which we agree!

The fifty-five-mile-an-hour limit is fine for the East Coast or in crowded cities, but it has no place in sparsely populated areas where the distances between towns is great. It is boring to drive long distances at safe speeds. Interstate highways are built for dangerously high speeds, so let's use them that way. Remember:

SPEED DOESN'T KILL PEOPLE,
BAD ACCIDENTS KILL PEOPLE.

Excuse me for now, I'm on my way to take part in a demonstration at an abortion clinic. I'm a stickler for the sanctity of life. (1986)

The Big Apple

The first report on that guy who did a Bronson to those kids in the New York subway was that he was acting in righteous revenge, that they'd tried to rip him off and he'd responded by pulling out a gun and shooting them.

Now it begins to look as though he may have gone into the subway looking for an excuse to use his gun, which changes the moral balance of the situation dramatically.

My fellow liberals are appalled; not merely that someone would do such a thing, but that the initial response of New Yorkers had been to regard the shooter as a hero, their champion.

New York Governor Mario Cuomo, the philosopher-king of knee-jerk liberalism, said:

"The vigilante spirit is dangerous and it's wrong. In the long run that's what produces the slaughter of innocent people."

Even New York Mayor Edward Koch, more of an Old Testament liberal, said:

"We will not permit people to take the law into their own hands. You are not going to have instant justice meted out by anybody, because that is not justice."

I can only suppose that neither of them has ridden the New York subway recently without a police escort.

Surely the transportation system in the inner circles of Dante's vision of hell must resemble that of New York. It is figuratively, as well as literally, a netherworld; a dimly lit, trash-filled dungeon traversed by rattling, graffiti-scarred trains where habitual riders sit stone faced—ignoring the stench, the cries of the mad, the blare of the stereos, the vacant stares of the junkies—lest an expression be mistaken for a welcoming sign or a challenge. Truly, it is a place for the damned.

You think I exaggerate? My daughter lives in New York. Whenever I visit her, she instructs me on proper subway behavior before she lets me go out alone.

"This is your rolled-up newspaper," she says in the manner of a Marine Corps drill instructor. "Get to know it. It is your best friend in case of attack."

"Attack?" I say. "What attack?"

"The subway isn't a Frank Capra movie, Dad. You've got to be prepared for anything."

She tells me that I must place my wallet in a front trouser pocket, nowhere else, or someone will snatch it. She herself would not so much as carry a purse onto a subway train. Or wear a necklace. She says that I must be careful not to stand anywhere near the edge of the platform or someone will push me into the path of an oncoming train.

"Why?" I ask her. "Why would someone push me in front of a train?"

She looks at me as though I belong in the slow learners' group. "Because it's the subway," she explains.

I read somewhere that New York is not the most dangerous city in the country and that there are statistics to support that assertion; but it is unrivaled among American cities for its projection of a sense of anarchy, a place where one's well-being depends not on a set of well-defined rules and regulations but on one's own resourcefulness. And the subway is perhaps the most extravagant expression of that characteristic.

To take the subway today is to experience a sense of menace, if not from one's fellow passengers, then from the system itself. The trains are old and rickety and the system is given to fires. Arson is suspected.

So what are they talking about, not letting people take the law into their own hands? What law?

The fellow they arrested for the shooting is obviously not the person you'd pick as an example; he may very well be a cuckoo. But what is a normal person to do on a subway or a street—and not just in New York, but anywhere—when some thug comes up to him and demands money?

Give it to him, right? That's the smart thing to do. It's even the liberal thing to do. It's only money.

But it isn't, you know. It's more than money; it's self-respect. You can't live at the mercy of thugs and maintain self-respect. Sometimes you have to stiffen your spine and say: "I'm mad as hell and I'm not going to take it anymore."

I think that's what the people of New York were saying with their immediate support of the gunman. They feel they are under attack by wild animals, and here was a story that said one of their own had bitten back—and they were glad.

We all know, deep down, that we can't let people go around shooting each other at will, no matter what their motives. The vigilante spirit is out of control even as it is activated.

But it's hard to remember that at times. Very hard. (1985)

The Big Apple II

The savage attack on the young woman running in New York's Central Park last week is one of those crimes that reaches deep into society's collective unconscious, exciting passions out of proportion to the magnitude of its tragedy.

After all, blameless people of great promise are killed and maimed each day all around us and we endure it handily, when we notice it. But the cruel fate of this one woman, set upon by a gang of youngsters—hardly more than children, really—has, against all odds, shocked the conscience of the nation. We stumble around trying to explain it, to find lessons in it, as if it would be less terrible if we could make sense of it.

If we could be sure that the gang members, all of whom are black or Hispanic, were victims of crushing poverty and the social chaos of the ghetto, we could blame racism. If they were thugs with long criminal records who had been set free by witless judges, we could blame the legal system. If they were addicted to dirty books and movies, we could blame pornography.

None of that seems to have been the case, at least not in an acute way. The attackers as best we can tell at this point were more middle class than not, most of them from intact homes where a certain amount of discipline was enforced. They had no record of thuggish behavior. None of the easy answers seem relevant or at least provable.

It's the very mindlessness of the crime that makes it so terrifying. It's as though the youngsters, who sang and laughed and joked in jail after their arrest, had committed an act of vandalism, on a human being instead of a building, with no real feeling for the distinction. One suspects that the victim could have been black or a man or poor and it would have made no difference. There was nothing personal about the attack, an impression heightened by the fact that the boys' backgrounds gave no warning of so monstrous an act. It's almost as though they were acting as agents for some larger force.

If we cannot identify that force as sociological or psychological, we are forced to accept the possibility that what we're dealing with is nothing less than Evil, an implacable force of darkness that beats like a heart just behind the flimsy facades of civilization we erect to mask our deeper natures. The attack then becomes an expression of something we all in greater or less degree share, and we are bound to that gang—as we are to lynch mobs, mass murderers, child abusers—by our common humanity. That is not an easy or pleasant thing to contemplate and so we look for answers elsewhere.

It has been suggested that we are wrong to blame the victim for her recklessness in running alone at night in northern Central Park, that she was merely asserting her right to live free. That proposition was stated most eloquently by the peerless Murray Kempton of *Newsday.* He wrote:

"We deny all meaning to her sacrifice at any moment when we decide that what she did was foolish. We cannot, of course, dispute the force of the event as an argument that her choice was incorrect, but it must not permit us to say that she was not right. We miss her point if we mistake her tragedy for no more than a prompting to caution.

"Cowardice is a poor companion and an even worse teacher, as courage is the best of both. She ran in the dark because she refused to lock her door twice, seal it with a bar and then huddle and shudder indoors. She preferred the open air to that too-common form of entombment. And hers is the only sound way to live."

To which one can only say: "Good writing Murray, but get real."

Central Park is just that, a park in the middle of Manhattan. It reaches from the Plaza Hotel on the south to Harlem on the north: from rich to poor, from white to color, from safe to dangerous. The Reservoir is a lake about two-thirds of the way up the park; the woman was attacked on a path north of the Reservoir.

Running in Central Park alone at night below the Reservoir is brave. Running in Central Park alone at night above the Reservoir is crazy.

There are times when it is necessary to confront Evil in order to confound it, times when it is possible, perhaps, to defeat it. But to feed oneself into its jaws as an act of bravado, just to prove you're not afraid, is foolhardy.

To defeat Evil it is first necessary to respect its power. (1989)

Human Nature

We call it, for want of a better name, the Holocaust, meaning the systematic slaughter of six million Jews and perhaps that many non-Jews in the German death camps of World War II. It is not a perfect name, perhaps, but it suggests the enormity of the event better than any other.

Millions of innocent people were herded into camps to live in indescribable misery and were subjected to torture, mutilation and starvation, with death the only escape. Death in all its forms came to the camps, but very often via mass executions that produced mountains of bodies that needed disposal. That's what the gas ovens were for: disposal. At times, though, it was necessary to resort to bulldozing the bodies into vast trenches. It is not an easy thing to get rid of twelve million people and be orderly about it.

The Holocaust was much with us last week, for it was the fortieth anniversary of the uprising in the Warsaw Ghetto when, for an instant, a group of doomed Jews offered armed resistance to their murderers. Groups of survivors of the camps met to commemorate the occasion, public television offered up documentaries and there were stories in newspapers and magazines and on public radio.

Very difficult stories, images: naked men and women being whipped to their graves by grinning Nazi guards; tangles of emaciated bodies with blank eyes staring out of faces caught by death in mid-scream; deep scratches on cinder block walls in gas chambers, where dying victims had clawed the walls for air.

I'd seen the films, or ones like them, before, but I watched again, almost against my will. The Holocaust remains as fascinating as it is horrifying. We ask ourselves, how could this thing have happened?

The short answer is "Nazis," I suppose, but that doesn't explain anything. The Holocaust cannot be explained by a political party.

Nor is the fascination simply a function of size. History is replete with great massacres, even attempts at genocide, some of which disappear from consciousness almost as soon as they happen. As recently as 1965, hundreds of thousands—perhaps millions—of Indonesians were murdered in a matter of a few weeks when a Communist coup failed. The event passed virtually unremarked. But not the Holocaust.

I think it stands as a dark shape on the horizon of our history, demanding explanation because it was an evil done to Jews—an articulate, literate people of great cultural attainment—by German Christians, no less articulate, no less literate, no less cultured. It was done, in short, to people much like ourselves, by people much like ourselves.

That's the astonishing part: that the Germany of Brahms and Schiller and Beethoven and Goethe could become that unspeakable monster—Nazi Germany.

We struggle with that paradox still, we of the West, and everyone arrives at his or her own interpretation. James Watt and his wife, Leilani, saw a film on the Holocaust in Washington last week. She said it showed how wrong abortion is and how much we need a strong defense. Watt said it showed the evils of centralized government. That seems to me bizarre, but my response to the film undoubtedly would be eccentric to them.

I was reminded of a statement made by Pope John Paul a month or so ago to the effect that atheism is the chief cause of evil in the world today. What could he have been thinking of? It seems closer to the truth to say that the two great sources of evil in the modern world are love of God and love of country—religion and nationalism. Almost all the truly great man-made disasters of our time can be traced to one or the other.

The Holocaust was the result of a merging of those two great forces in Germany. I do not think that Germans killed Jews in spite of the fact that they, the Germans, were Christians, but because they were.

It is one of the geniuses of the American system of government that we keep these two great emotional forces apart in our society.

Does that mean I think the lesson of the Holocaust is separation of church and state? Not really. The event is too grand in its malevolence to admit to glib, easy lessons.

Were I to choose a single observation most consistent with the facts of history, however, it would be that of Rabbi Seymour Siegel, director of the United States Holocaust Memorial Council:

"The human heart is evil above all things." (1983)

10

CANCEL MY APPOINTMENT
IN SAMARA

I KNOW WAR. I came very close to giving my life for my country during the Korean war. I was serving in the U.S. Naval Reserve on the "attack transport" S.S. Rockbridge. I'll never know why they called it an attack transport; we couldn't have attacked an armed inner tube. Still, we had those World War II anti-aircraft guns and every once in a while we would practice firing them.

I say "we." I was in college and in the inactive reserve, hiding out from the war. I attended meetings at home once a week and every summer went out on a two-week training mission. (Some day I'd like to trade war stories with Dan Quayle.) The Rockbridge was that summer's training mission.

The gunnery practice consisted of trying to hit a wind sock pulled by a low-flying plane that looked like a Flying Jenny. It seemed to travel at about sixty miles an hour. It would drone by and we would shoot at it copiously, seldom hitting anything.

Generally speaking the regular sailors handled the shooting, but one day they decided to give the reserves a chance. My job was to take clips of shells out of the ammunition boxes and hand them to a sailor who stuck them into the gun.

The first clip I pulled out came apart in my hand and in a moment loose shells, each the size of a loaf of French bread, were bouncing on the deck.

"Duck!" I remember the gun chief yelling. "The son-of-a-bitch is trying to kill us all." We all dove for cover (son-of-a-bitch included), but the shells didn't go off. I was relieved of my duties in disgrace and relief.

So I know war, give or take. Which is why I never advocate it.

I'm not a full-blown pacifist but I find war so monumentally stu-pid and wasteful, whatever its circumstances, that I think everything else should be tried at least twice before resorting to combat.

Which should explain why I felt the way I did about the "holy war" against Saddam Hussein:

August, War Rises

I'm starting to wish we hadn't called George Bush a wimp so many times. It was bad enough to have him chew pork rinds and pitch horse-shoes, if he starts trying to prove his manhood against Saddam Hus-sein it could get unhealthy for children and other living things.

Not that I'm against waging war against Iraq in principle, you understand. In the abstract, I am a hawk. As a loyal, patriotic Ameri-can, I will support my president in any armed conflict right up until actual fighting breaks out. The problem is, war in the actual seldom if ever lives up to the promise of war in the abstract.

Which means I'm getting a little nervous. It's beginning to look as though armed conflict is about to break out. I took that message when Mr. Bush, in a speech to the Veterans of Foreign Wars the other day, quoted Dwight Eisenhower's address to the troops on D-day.

"The eyes of the world are upon you," Bush quoted. "The hopes and prayers of liberty-loving people everywhere march with you. Let us all beseech the blessing of almighty God upon this great and noble undertaking."

Somehow that quotation, first uttered in the service of the crusade against the Nazi war machine, loses something when applied to the defense of the sheiks of Araby.

I'll tell you the truth: When this thing started a few weeks ago I didn't think it was going to come to war. War is always a dumb, un-economical way to settle an economic conflict; it costs more than it's worth.

But, when you think about it, when did that ever stop a war? As two sides face off with ever-increasing forces and the rhetoric becomes more shrill, it becomes more probable that things will turn out badly. Which is where we are now.

I still believe we can win a war with Iraq but perhaps not as easily as I first thought. And, in any case, suppose we do defeat Saddam once and for all, what then? What sort of New World Order can be expected to rise from the resultant chaos? It is entirely possible that we win the war and find control of our precious oil supply in even more unstable hands. This is security?

War always has unlooked-for results. Take Panama. We invaded Panama to bring to justice Manuel Noriega, dictator and drug baron. By doing so we would not only put him out of commission, we would strike terror into the hearts of drug king-pins through Central and South America, immobilizing them. That was our reasoning.

The other day the *New York Times* carried a story on how things are going in Panama since we knocked off ol' Pineapple Face. Badly; that's how they're going.

Drug trafficking, freed from the iron hand of Noriega's corrupt control, has gotten worse. Smugglers now have virtually unlimited access to the many rural landing strips and coastal areas and they are taking advantage of it.

"The size of the problem is really frightening," said the head of the Panama customs agency. A foreign diplomat added: "It's not so much a question of corruption. The government is just outmanned, outgunned and outmaneuvered."

So much for our primary objective. But what of the cost? The casualty figures on the invasion are murky. We say we killed 202 Panamanian civilians and 50 of Noriega's troops. A respected human rights monitoring group puts the civilian death toll at 300 and the wounded at 3,000. Others claim the deaths run into the thousands.

In addition—or is it subtraction?—the bombing we gave Panama City produced 15,000 homeless. And before we're out of it the bill for Operation Just Cause, the rather droll name the Pentagon thought up for the invasion, will amount to hundreds of millions of dollars.

And what do we have to show for all of it? One tin-horn dictator in an American cell, facing a rap which he stands a good chance of beating.

Whatever you thought of it as theater, as policy the invasion of Panama was a disaster.

This, too, is what I fear of a war with Iraq, win or lose. We will do the fighting and Japan and Germany and France will sit back and reap the rewards. It seems to me I've seen this movie before.

Damn me for a Nervous Nellie if you will, but I don't like the look of it. (1990)

November, War Threatens

If George Bush is running a bluff, it's a beauty. I don't know whether he's convinced Saddam Hussein that we're going to attack him, but he's convinced me. I think we're going to war.

Congress is milling about and making noises about wanting to be consulted but basically it will go along with whatever the president decides. It's either that or assuming its constitutional responsibilities and that would break recent precedents.

It's not as though we don't have a reason for being in the Persian Gulf, after all. We have a dozen of them. The problem is that none of them are good reasons. Here is just a sampling of the ones that have surfaced so far:

• **We're protecting our way of life**—President Bush said that but didn't explain what he meant. He couldn't have meant our way of life as an embodiment of justice, freedom and representative democracy, since the countries we're protecting don't have any of those things. And if he meant our way of life as expressed in everybody driving around alone in his or her car, that hardly seems a good enough reason to spend tens of thousands of lives.

• **We've got to save Kuwait from ravages of the Iraqi invasion force**—A noble aim, but it's a little late for that. Kuwait has already been raped, looted and pillaged to a turn. In any case, it seems unlikely that door-to-door street fighting by two extravagantly equipped armies will improve the lot of the Kuwaitis.

• **We can't let naked aggression go unchecked**—The truth is, we can. We do it all the time. If we cranked up our armed forces every time some country attacked its neighbor—naked or clothed— we'd have to start drafting lawyers and stock brokers for cannon fodder. Iraqi has done nothing to Kuwait that China, for example, has not done to Tibet, and we've lived with that just fine, thank you very much.

• **Saddam is Hitler**—I question the usefulness of labeling every two-bit thug with an attitude problem a new Hitler. Khadafy was a Hitler, Noriega was a Hitler, now it's Saddam's turn. Listen, I remember Hitler. Hitler was an enemy of mine. Saddam Hussein is no Hitler. He's more like Al Capone with missiles.

• **Saddam is Herbert Hoover**—The other day Secretary of State James Baker suggested that Saddam, unless checked, would cause unemployment. Speaking of the consequences to the United States of the Iraqi invasion, he said: "To bring it down to the level of the average American citizen, let me say that means jobs. If you want to sum it up in one word, it's jobs." It may be the first time a United States secretary of state justified a war as a jobs program. Do you notice how life is beginning to imitate Dan Quayle?

• **Saddam will soon have The Bomb**—Perhaps true, but you have to ask yourself how he got it. He bought the technology and spare parts from Western corporations who are perfectly willing to sell a nuclear holocaust to any lunatic with the price. Having been unwilling to inconvenience these corporations in their pursuit of a dollar or mark, it hardly seems fair to have young men and women lay down their lives to undo their work. You don't need 400,000 troops to stop nuclear proliferation, you need political will.

Then, of course, there's that other theory, the one based on coincidence.

What a coincidence, the theory goes, that just at the moment of the collapse of the Communist threat, rendering our $300 billion-a-year military budget obsolescent, another threat pops up.

And more of a coincidence that when Iraqi troops massed on the borders of Kuwait, our State Department went out of its way to announce that we had no defense treaty with Kuwait, while our Iraqi ambassador was telling Saddam himself: "We have no opinion on the Arab-Arab conflicts, like your border disagreements with Kuwait." Eight days later he attacked and suddenly he was Hitler.

At which point the military budget, which was on the verge of being politically unsupportable, became supportable again. As Defense Secretary Dick Cheney likes to say: "It's a dangerous world out there." Yes, dangerous and full of coincidence.

I personally would not suggest that President Bush and the people who pull his strings suckered Saddam into succumbing to his worst instincts just to keep the military-industrial complex fed. Perish the thought. That would be cynical.

Just once before we go to war, though, I wish they'd tell us exactly what in hell we're doing over there and make it convincing. (1990)

December, War Looms

The more you think about it and the more you hear the Bush flunkies explain it, the more obvious it becomes that putting 400,000 American troops in the desert is a truly loopy idea, right up there with building a fence across South Vietnam to keep the North Vietnamese home.

The only dumber idea I can conceive of is sending them across the desert to attack Saddam Hussein in his stronghold.

We've got this guy where we want him, surrounded and isolated. The only thing he's got to sell is oil and we won't let him sell it. He is an ice cream cone melting in the sun. It's only a matter of time before he is a puddle on the floor. Why would we want to give up our advantage and fight him on his own terms?

I listened to Defense Secretary Dick Cheney and Joint Chiefs Chairman Colin Powell trying to justify an invasion to the Senate Armed Services Committee the other day. It was embarrassing. Their reasoning wouldn't pass muster in a fraternity bull session. For example:

Cheney said the coalition arrayed against Saddam might disintegrate if we wait around too long before we attacked. This would be a disaster, he said, because Saddam is a terrible threat to his neighbors and the rest of the world.

You can't have it both ways. If Saddam is such a threat to the rest of the world, why should the coalition disintegrate? Does Mr. Bush think the rest of the world isn't smart enough to figure out what's threatening it and what's not?

Cheney also said that the embargo is hurting our economy and those of some of our allies, particularly Turkey. True, but easily corrected. Saudi Arabia and the other Arab Gulf states are earning tens of billions of dollars in excess profits as a result of the embargo of Iraq. Since they are the primary beneficiaries of the embargo doesn't it seem fair to expect them to indemnify the rest of the coalition against economic loss? If they don't want to do it, we can always pick up our troops and go home and let them haggle with Saddam on their own.

Powell, our Gilbert and Sullivan general, said he wasn't sure the embargo will achieve our goal; namely, getting rid of Saddam. As it happens, two of his predecessors, General David Jones and Admiral William Crowe, disagreed.

"If in fact the sanctions will work in twelve to eighteen months instead of six months," said Crowe, "the trade-off of avoiding war with its attendant sacrifices and uncertainties would, in my view, be worth it." That might sound self-evident to you, but it comes as fresh information to the Bush people.

What about Saddam getting The Bomb, you say? There's a simple answer to that.

Bomb Switzerland.

German customs, according to the *New York Times'* resident hawk William Safire, recently discovered an illegal shipment of strategic metal headed for Iraq from Switzerland, metal that could be used in the construction of an atom bomb.

So bomb the Swiss factory making it. It would not only deprive Saddam of the metal, it would send a message to the other western manufacturers who are supplying him with a nuclear capability. Stop doing it: that's the message.

The Swiss would probably get cranky, of course, but so what? What are they going to do, stop sending us watches?

All else aside, a couple of things keep bothering me.

Why did Reagan and Bush systematically dismantle Jimmy Carter's policy to make us energy self-sufficient, pursuing instead an active policy of making us more dependent on Gulf oil so that we became more vulnerable to the volatile politics of the Middle East?

Why did Kuwait ignore OPEC quotas and increase its production of oil last spring, driving the price down and pushing Iraq, with its enormous war debts, to the edge of economic collapse? What or who gave that tiny country the arrogance to refuse to negotiate the matter with its powerful, bellicose neighbor when it protested? And why did our ambassador encourage Saddam in his territorial ambitions by telling him that we were neutral in the matter of Arab-Arab border disputes?

There is a scene in the musical play *Guys and Dolls* in which the "oldest established permanent floating crap game in New York" takes to the sewers to escape the police, and one of the players, Big Julie from Chicago, produces his own dice in an effort to change his luck. The other players notice that the dice have no spots on them.

"That's okay," says Big Julie. "I got 'em memorized."

That's the way I feel now. We are playing with George Bush's blank dice and he's got the spots memorized. Somebody does, anyway. (1990)

January—Bingo!

So much for sending a message to Saddam.

In last week's congressional debate on the war, speaker after speaker argued that we had to convince Saddam that we were serious, that it was our only chance to avoid war. Jim Leach, a liberal Republican from Iowa, said: "I am personally convinced Saddam has no choice except to blink before the 15th—unless America blinks first."

Some blink. The lesson, I think, is that when you vote for war, war is what you get.

And war is what we have, a serious war that is being taken seriously. You saw hardly a smile on the streets of Washington Thursday. There was no visible joy even at the reports of our early success.

Which is altogether appropriate. War is too somber a matter to be entered into joyously.

Having said that, let me say also that if those early reports are to be believed, we had an astonishing first day. One thousand sorties with two planes lost! That's not combat, that's a World War II movie. You would think you'd drop more than two planes just flying around.

And how do you surprise an enemy when you tell him pretty much when you're going to attack? For two months now we've been saying, "Saddam, you've got until January 15, then the balloon goes up." So the sun goes down on January 16, we send our planes over and Saddam thinks it's a sneak attack.

I'm beginning to believe, and not for the first time, that Saddam Hussein is a Proposition 48 dictator. He needs some remedial courses before he's ready to play for the varsity.

Almost as remarkable as our lack of casualties is the apparent fact that we actually hit the targets we were aiming at. This may turn out to be the first air attack in history that deserved the name "surgical air strike." The story of the Iraqi defense ministry building in Baghdad being hit by three bombs while the civilian area around it remains untouched is nothing short of amazing, almost too good to be true.

If the reports do hold up, however, we have the greatest air force ever assembled and perhaps the greatest fighting force and I take back all the nasty things I've said about overpriced American military hardware.

How about going the sanctions route now? I mean it. We've achieved most of our goals or are in the process of doing so. We're destroying Saddam's poison gas factories, his ability to build a bomb, much of his offensive capability. Bomb him another week and he will be no threat to any neighbor.

So why not just throw an embargo on Iraq—not let anything in or out—and wait for the creep to disappear? In other words, do not send our troops crashing across the desert to assault his entrenched positions in Kuwait and Iraq. I know, that's not George Bush's style, and he's got the bit in his teeth now, but if he can get out of this without suffering great casualties he would be a great hero and deserve to be.

George Bush has done a very bold thing. He has taken all the chips of his presidency and moved them into the center of the table. From the very first he has placed his bet on war and on a short, relatively painless war at that. If he wins, he's going to win big. If he loses, however, there's no bottom to it. This might be a good time to hedge the bet little.

I'm aware of the futility of saying things like that. The president is going to do what he's going to do and the rest of us are merely along for the ride.

At this point, as in any war, good information is hard to come by and opinions based on the information available not worth much. No matter what the eventual outcome it will take months and perhaps years to figure out what it truly means.

I think of Robert Southey's poem "After Blenheim." Southey, an early nineteenth century poet laureate of England, writes of two children, Peterkin and Wilhelmine, who find a skull in the field on which, years before, the battle of Blenheim was fought. They ask their grandfather about the battle. He answers, in part:

> *They say it was a shocking sight*
>   *After the field was won;*
> *For many thousand bodies here*
>   *Lay rotting in the sun;*
> *But things like that, you know, must be*
> *After a famous victory . . . .*
>
> *And everybody praised the Duke*
>   *Who this great fight did win.*
> *"But what good came of it at last?"*
>   *Quoth little Peterkin:—*
> *Why, that I cannot tell, said he,*
> *But 'twas a famous victory!*

Let us pray, then, for a victory as lasting as it is famous, but a victory in any case. Win or lose, win is better. (1991)

But First, Let's Kill All the Lawyers

If we're going to have a war there's little sense in whining about it. You don't want people calling you a Nervous Nellie or thinking you're lacking in manhood (or womanhood, for that matter).

I made the mistake of insufficient enthusiasm for the war in Vietnam and paid the price. I was pilloried by my betters (and worsts) and shunned by the people who threw the best dinner parties in Washington. I'm not going to make that mistake again. I'm going to spend this war as a hawk.

I know, I've said this was an unnecessary war and President Bush should be dragged through bramble for getting us into it, but that was then. Now is now and I'm for the war. With slight modifications.

For openers, I think it's essential that we reinstitute the draft. It's one thing to con young people into the armed forces by telling them to "be all they can be"; it's another when all they can be is dead. A draft is a much fairer way to supply our military with missile fodder, provided it's conducted in a fair way.

To that end I would not have a draft lottery which, under the best of circumstances, merely spreads the unfairness around in a haphazard way. I would instead first draft those who have benefited most from our society—middle-aged professionals and business leaders. Yes, I know, you'd have to reject quite a few of them on medical grounds but, with the physical fitness craze and all, not so many as you might think. It's a mechanized army, after all. The point is, the ones who passed the physical would make great soldiers.

As James Stregenga, the Purdue history professor who inspired this idea, said a dozen years ago:

"Instead of calling up a couple hundred thousand immature nineteen-year-olds . . . who will have to be mothered and socialized to accept the rigors of military life, the military could draft emotionally mature fifty-year-olds who have spent their adult lives working in organizations, patiently coping, understanding and accepting legitimate restrictions, suffering idiots, and shouldering responsibilities . . . .

"Ask yourself whom you'd rather go into combat with; the gawky kid down the street who recently barely graduated from high school, or your grownup corner grocer who used to be a truck mechanic?"

And that's only one advantage of the plan. If the worst should happen and our middle-aged warrior buys the Big Casino, he or she will be less missed than their younger counterparts who very often leave behind small children. In Stregenda's words: "It's better (or at least not as sad) for fifty-year-olds to miss their last twenty years than for twenty-year-olds to miss their last fifty."

Again, sound thinking.

He doesn't go far enough, however. The ideal patriot is not merely middle-aged but successful. Who, after all, is better suited to the role of super patriot than one who has tasted the sweetest fruit this great country has to offer?

For that reason I think we should draft lawyers before we draft anyone else, concentrating particularly on those who think *pro bono* is Cher's former brother-in-law. If society gives you a license to steal, the least you should be prepared to do is die for it.

Politicians would come next; it was their inattention, after all, that allowed matters to come to this. They will undoubtedly be happy to make good on their errors of judgment.

After them, newspaper columnists—especially those who feel that America's position in the world demands it act as a global sheriff's posse. Then bankers, corporation executives and stock brokers, most of whom are either unnecessary to a just society or a hindrance to it.

I would limit the drafting of doctors to those who own their own X-ray machines and use them to run up their patients' bills.

There are other possibilities, but that's a start. I'll tell you, I would not mind going to this stupid war myself if I could look up and down the ranks of my fellow soldiers and see the likes of Dan Quayle, Michael Milken, George Will, Newt Gingrich and Elliot Abrams, patriots who excused themselves from the Vietnam hostilities.

I think Saddam Hussein would be impressed too. If he knew he was up against a foe so committed to victory that its middle-aged professionals were willing to offer up their decaying bodies for the cause of a New World Order, he would think twice about staying in Kuwait. He might even surrender.

In any case, it would be a gesture of warlike sincerity virtually unparalleled in modern times. (1991)

Casualty Report

There is a saying, credited to Senator Hiram Johnson, the great California populist, in 1917: "The first casualty when war comes is truth." A smart man, that Johnson.

Truth is the enemy of war always, and to seek it in wartime is to risk being branded a traitor. During the Civil War, Union General George Meade objected to dispatches filed by a Philadelphia reporter, so he had the gentleman placed backward on a horse, with a sign saying "Libeler of the Press" around his neck, and paraded through the troops to the tune of "Rogue's March." By some reports, the Bush people would like to do that to CNN's Peter Arnett right now for his dispatches from Baghdad.

The name of the game in warfare is to convince your countrymen that they are being defended by King Arthur and his Knights of the Roundtable while the enemy is made up of sub-human villains without a shred of decency to veil their depravity.

Muhammar Khadafy was a terrible guy; that's why he had to be bombed. Same with Manuel Noriega. If we hadn't killed hundreds of people to arrest him, there's no telling what would have happened. We might even have a drug problem. Now it's Saddam.

There's a book *The First Casualty* by Phillip Knightley that chronicles the reporting of war over the past 150 years. If wars are not all alike, they at least begin alike, with the demonization of the enemy.

Perhaps the most famous example is the Rape of Belgium stories that surfaced in 1914 at the outset of World War I. German troops were pictured in the British press as barbarians who took pleasure in the bayonetting of children and the gang-raping of young virgins. A blue-ribbon commission of lawyers and historians was formed quickly to study the charges. It found them all to be true. The world was shocked and a war which had seemed to many Britains a European squabble, best avoided, became a conflict between good and evil.

In 1922, after the slaughter of nine million troops and God knows how many civilians, a Belgian commission of inquiry was unable to corroborate a single major atrocity listed in the 1915 report.

George Bush, in his own gee-whiz-golly way, has tried to demonize Saddam Hussein. He puffed up in righteous indignation the other day when, in a speech to the Reserve Officers Association, he said:

"Saddam has sickened the world with his use of Scud missiles—those inaccurate bombs that indiscriminately strike at cities and innocent civilians, in both Israel and Saudi Arabia. These weapons are nothing more than tools of terror, and they do nothing but strengthen our resolve to act against a dictator unmoved by human decency."

Bush really has no talent for exciting emotions. Saddam uses inaccurate bombs; what a tyrant.

There is a case to be made against Saddam's use of indiscriminate weapons on a civilian population, but President Bush isn't the one to make it. Where was he during the Vietnam War, when—forget My Lai—we dropped tons of flechette bombs on villages, sending dartlike shrapnel into the flesh of men, women and children alike? The darts were contrived as fishhooks, so as to be almost impossible to remove.

I don't recall George Bush railing against the sickening viciousness of that.

Frankly, I'm willing to concede the fact that Saddam is a cruel and pitiless despot, but that's not why we have engaged him in war. He is no more cruel or pitiless now than he was when he was our ally, and his ruthlessness does not exceed that of other leaders whose good opinion we pursue. We fight for oil; make no mistake about it.

And if we now indulge our best instincts in the conduct of the war—taking care not to target civilians—that, too, will change. As the war drags on, assuming that it does, we will become less fastidious. In war as in football, "Winning isn't the most important thing; it's the only thing." To be unmoved by considerations of human decency is the nature of modern warfare.

But most of us don't want to hear that. We want to know that we are embarked on an honorable cause against a heinous foe in a fight not of our making. That is what countries always want to know in a war and that is what they are always told; both sides.

Even by the extravagant standards set so far, however, I thought sending Dan Quayle to military bases to "comfort" the families of our troops in the Middle East set new records for brazen hypocrisy.

On the other hand, there are few people who know more about

being comfortable during a war, so maybe it was the right choice. (1991)

Simpspeak

The White House sicced its No. 1 junkyard dog on Peter Arnett last week. Given this administration's commitment to the First Amendment, the only real surprise is that it took so long.

Arnett, of course, is the Pulitzer Prize winning journalist whose daily reports from Baghdad on CNN are driving the propaganda patriots in the White House up the wall. His reporting of the damage done the city by our bombing raids has dimmed the luster of the White House fairy tales that our bombs are so smart they strike only military targets, leaving civilians untouched. As it turns out civilians are being touched, sometimes to the point of being killed.

So the White House rolled out its Senate minority whip, Alan (The Wyoming Whiner) Simpson, whose talent for mean-spirited vituperation is exceeded only by his contempt for the truth.

Simpson accused Arnett of being an enemy sympathizer, not only in this war but in Vietnam, saying that one of Arnett's brothers-in-law was a Viet Cong.

As it happens none of that is true but it hasn't deterred Simpson from continuing his assault on Arnett. He denies that the White House put him up to it but, with his track record of carrying dirty water for the administration, the denial inspires skepticism.

But forget all of that. Arnett shouldn't have to be responsible for his brothers-in-law, nor is the motivation of an administration toady like Simpson an issue. The point is, Arnett has been doing great work in difficult circumstances in Baghdad—measured, careful, honest reporting—which is more than you can say for most of the correspondents on our side of the line.

This has, so far, been the most poorly covered war in my lifetime. The word of the military command is generally taken as holy writ. Interviews with soldiers must be conducted in the presence of a military flack. All other news is filtered through censored pool reports. It has been one long Pentagon briefing.

This, of course, is what the White House wants. It allows it to continue the charade that this is a no-cost war. Our allies are paying for it, we are suffering minimal casualties and we are killing only bad guys.

Arnett and now the other reporters who have been let into Baghdad give lie to that conceit. You can't go into a war like this wearing a white suit and expect to come out the other side without a mark.

We have killed innocents in this war and will continue to do so. We're going to kill pregnant women and children and old people and sick people. We are, in fact, going to do all the terrible things that Saddam did when he invaded Kuwait, the things that made him a modern-day Hitler. It's the nature of modern warfare. If we can't accept that, we shouldn't have bought chips in this game in the first place.

The things I miss most about the reporting so far is the perspective of Willy and Joe, Bill Mauldin's scruffy, war-wise, dog-faced soldiers of World War II, who were cynical about their officers and unpersuaded that the army was infallible. In their stead we get flyboys or gung-ho kids who seem to believe all the crap they're being fed.

Perhaps the unhappy Simpson should consider a move to England, home to the most jingoistic press in the world and the one least critical of its government's military adventures.

It doesn't even bother to shield its true feelings behind the sanctimony of "just war" theology. For example, last month a famous British conservative columnist, Sir Peregrine Worsthorne (say what you want about the Brits, they have great names), wrote:

"It is beginning to look as if Saddam Hussein has given the West a chance once again to establish its unchallengeable pre-eminence in a manner impregnable at once to moral obloquy and military resistance. Not only will our arms have prevailed in a most spectacular fashion. So also will our ideals.

"Nothing is ever forever. Sooner or later the Third World will throw up other challenges. But if the Gulf war ends as it has begun, there can be no doubt who are the masters now—at any rate for another generation.

"We have the laser beams and they have not. And the we who

matter are not the Germans or the Japanese or the Russians but the Americans. Happy days are here again. Bliss it is in this dawn to be alive; but to be an old reactionary is very heaven."

Which is undoubtedly what Alan Simpson would say about the war were he better educated and not so resolute a hypocrite. (1991)

Is It War, Or Is It Memorex?

Leave it to television. It trivializes everything, even war. Our noble enterprise to establish a New World Order, nip a new Hitler in the bud and restore freedom, justice, democracy and long lunch hours to Kuwait has degenerated into a video game.

"Play Top Gun, Junior. Put the building in the cross hairs. Push the button. POW! See the debris fly out the windows. Here is a commercial to help you forget about what's in the debris."

We have entered the "war is heck" era of combat reporting. There's something definitely creepy about sitting around our living rooms watching armies clash between commercials. And if we worry that watching pornography leads to sex, why don't we worry about what watching war leads to?

The film they've shown on the high-tech bombing has been mesmerizing—putting bombs in doorways, for crying out loud—but, when you come down to it, it's just television. You still don't know what it all means. We don't know whether we'll be better off for it or not; we just know we can do it.

I'll tell you one thing, though; Mr. Bush doesn't have to worry about me getting euphoric. I'm not euphoric.

There are no harmless wars. People, even people called "debris," die in war, and the killing does not stop when they cut to a commercial.

It's a curious set of values we adopt in wartime. I was vaguely sickened by the pictures of the captured allied pilots, battered and demoralized, whom Saddam paraded about. Such treatment of prisoners was in violation of the Geneva Convention as President Bush, quivering with outrage, rightly pointed out.

Yet, had the Iraqis *killed* the same pilots in the air, rather than capturing them, that would have been fine. There's no convention against killing enemy soldiers, only treating them badly. Weird.

But no weirder, actually, than the concept of sacrifice we bring to war. We're willing to send our young men and women off to fight every time the president says our honor has been offended, and we punch out the first traitor who fails to support our troops. But don't ask us to reach into our pockets and make that support tangible.

H. Ross Perot, the nation's wisest rich person, has spent the past several months talking to business leaders. At last count he had spoken to 15,000 since the August 2 invasion of Kuwait. He reports:

"I ask every group whether they are ready to go to war. Particularly early on, everybody was rocking to do it.

"Then I ask how many have sons and daughters in the Middle East. So far it's been eight out of 15,000. So I say, 'It's the people who work for you who have children over there.' Okay.

"So we can agree we ought to have a system of daily sacrifice here so we can be emotionally committed to our troops, right? The only way for that is a war tax. How many for that?

"Zero of 15,000."

That's shocking. Lester Thurow, the MIT economist, made a useful distinction between an establishment and an oligarchy in a recent article.

An establishment, he said, was a ruling class that felt it's well-being was dependent to a greater or lesser degree on the well-being of society, and acted accordingly, while an oligarchy was a ruling class that felt it could prosper without regard to the rest of society. And it, too, acted accordingly.

It seems that we are indeed becoming a society run by a ruling class whose motto is: "I'm all right, Jack; I've got mine."

South America, here we come.

On one thing we can all agree, however, I think. The silliest argument of the war so far is over whether they should cancel the Super Bowl because there's a war going on. Of course they shouldn't cancel the Super Bowl.

They should cancel the war. (1991)

The BIG Stick

Last week Defense Secretary Dick Cheney said that we were keeping our options open with regard to the use of nuclear force in the Persian Gulf. That is the sanitized way of saying: "If push comes to shove, we just might nuke the creeps."

That shocked some people. Not me. Others thought it was simply an idle threat to give Saddam something to think about. Not me.

I think that we could very well wind up using atomic weapons against Iraqi forces. And, as a flag-waving, support-the-president hawk on this war, I'm all for it; the sooner the better.

I can just see all of you ultra-liberal, animal-rightist, vegetarian, ban-The-Bomb peaceniks recoiling in horror. *Oh no, not The Bomb; not that!* No wonder you never win an election.

Atomic weapons are not different in kind from guns, knives or bits of sharp metal, they differ merely in degree. The sentimental notion that killing people wholesale is somehow morally inferior to killing them retail will not stand the scrutiny of logical analysis. People, once they're dead, do not much care how they got that way. Kill is kill; dead is dead. The only thing you have to worry about when you kill people in war is whether God is on your side and, fortunately for us in this instance, He is. Would the president lie?

Here are only a few of the arguments for making Baghdad Hiroshima's sister city:

• **It would save time.** At the rate it's going now, this war might drag on for months, sending the economy over the edge of recession into the trough of depression. Speaking of which, it's pretty depressing to have the war in your living room every time you turn on the television. A bomb could restore prosperity and our good humor in a flash.

• **It would save American lives.** The first ground skirmish, hardly more than a fender-bender, cost us a dozen lives or so, and we killed more of them than Saddam did. A long war could mean casualty lists that resurrect the worst days of Vietnam. A well-placed nuclear strike would bring our troops home relatively unscarred. Iraqis would die in great numbers, of course, but that's the price you pay for having the wrong god on your side.

• **It would save the environment.** We've had a glimpse of what a protracted war in Iraq and Kuwait will mean: massive oil spills, continent-wide air pollution, the destruction of oil wells, contaminated water, potholes. You drop an atom bomb and you contain all of your pollution in one place. One hole takes care of it all; particularly if you don't count the radioactive cloud. Sure, it would make the site uninhabitable, but Iraq isn't all that inhabitable anyway.

• **It would punish aggression.** We're in this thing to promote a New World Order, right? We're trying to make an object lesson of Mr. Saddam so that other brutal dictators will not be tempted to commit naked aggression against their neighbors. What better way to teach Saddam a lesson than to vaporize him?

• **It would cut military spending.** Once the world became persuaded that we not only had nuclear weapons, we were willing to use them, we wouldn't need a vast army and all the little gimcracks that go with it. The rest of the nations would invite us to their parties, laugh at all our jokes, and let us run the New World Order out of respect. If not respect, fear. We wouldn't even need more nuclear weapons, having put in a lifetime supply already. We could cut the defense budget from $300 billion to $1.78, plus gas money and walk-around change for a few button-pushers.

• **And, finally, it would relieve us of the burden of our hypocritical posturing.** We're trying to have things both ways right now. We're attempting to portray ourselves as nice guys and win a war at the same time. That's nonsense. There is no way to wage war cleanly or morally or with honor. You simply win or lose, and if you win, you're a nation of heroes; if you lose, you're a nation of war criminals. There's no inbetween. If you can't justify using nuclear weapons in a war, you can't justify the war at all. If we are truly defending our vital interests, then we are justified in using any means at our disposal to do so. That's why we call them "vital" interests. If, on the other hand, it is merely convenient for us to win this war, then we should seek other means to get rid of Saddam. A war of convenience isn't worth the blood and treasure we'll be spending on it. (1991)

On the Eve of Destruction

The word from our military honchos is that a ground attack on Iraqi forces is "not imminent." They're saying it'll be three or four more weeks before we move. I wouldn't bet on that.

I suspect that the great fear of our army commanders is that the war will end before they can send in troops and demonstrate how necessary they are, thereby protecting their appropriation, not to mention their jobs.

Does that sound excessively cynical? It shouldn't.

It is no accident that every military venture of recent years, no matter how piddling, has involved *all* the armed forces, often to the detriment of the venture. Let the air force or the navy win a war all by itself just once and, by God, those fools on the Hill might decide that we don't need an army.

That, I can only conclude, must be what's behind President Bush continuing to claim that you can't drive the Iraqis out of Kuwait without a ground war. It's perfectly obvious that you can, of course.

All you have to do is use your unchallenged air power to keep Iraq from resupplying its troops in Kuwait. Sooner or later they will either have to surrender or try a suicidal breakout. It's a kind of industrial strength sanctions policy.

To say that you own the skies but are unable to starve out the enemy flies in the face of reason.

A ground war, of course, will produce casualties, but I imagine the planners are confident that they can bleed the Iraqis sufficiently with bombing to ensure a quick victory and keep those casualties at a minimum. That's the art of it; bringing the enemy to the brink of collapse with air power, but leaving something for the army. One can only hope that their timing is exquisite.

In any case, the casualty issue is overrated. Generals do not gain glory and a place in history by holding down casualties. If that were true the most famous general of the Civil War would be the North's

George McClellan, a man of utmost caution who was celebrated chiefly for his reluctance to fight.

Historian Shelby Foote, in his marvelous *The Civil War: A Narrative,* writes that McClellan advanced in battle "with something of the manner of a man walking on slippery ice through a darkness filled with wolves."

The great heroes of the Civil War, on the other hand, were thunderbolts like Grant and Lee, ruthless in their willingness to hurl their troops into the jaws of death. As Confederate General Nathan Bedford Forrest said: "War means fighting. And fighting means killing."

Stonewall Jackson, another great hero, was equally candid. He once overheard a subordinate expressing admiration for the bravery of Union troops he had fought that day and regret at having to reward such courage with slaughter.

"No," said Jackson. "Shoot them all. I do not wish them to be brave."

Perhaps the most eloquent critic of war, as well as one of its most relentless practitioners, was Union General William Tecumseh Sherman. He was superintendent at Louisiana State Military Academy when the war broke out, to the enthusiastic huzzahs of his colleagues. In exasperation and bitterness, he told them:

"You people of the South don't know what you are doing. This country will be drenched in blood, and God only knows how it will end. It is all folly, madness, a crime against civilization! You people speak so lightly of war; you don't know what you're talking about. War is a terrible thing!"

And he made sure that it was. Years later, when he had captured Atlanta and ordered it evacuated of civilians, he responded to the Atlanta mayor's protest that the order would inflict hardship and suffering on the sick and aged.

"You cannot qualify war in harsher terms than I will," he said. "War is cruelty, and you cannot refine it . . . You might as well appeal against the thunderstorm as against those terrible hardships of war." He evacuated the city—and burned it when he left.

Some fifteen years after the war, in a speech to a military academy, he said:

"I am tired and sick of war. Its glory is all moonshine. It is only those who have neither fired a shot nor heard the shrieks and groans of the wounded who cry aloud for blood, more vengeance, more desolation. War is hell."

Our General Schwarzkopf, Stormin' Norman, says that Sherman is one of his great heroes. I hope so. I have a feeling that if Sherman could have won a battle with air power and spared his troops, he would have done it and appropriations be damned. (1991)

Ten days later, the ground war began.

A hundred hours later, it was over.

The Unhappy Few

It was heartbreaking to see the survivors, eyes glazed from weeks of being pounded by enemy fire, staggering out of their shelters to fall on their knees and kiss the hands of their captors. One particularly pathetic group formed a semicircle and began to chant: "Tsorge Boosh, Tsorge Boosh, Tsorge Boosh." That's the last meeting of the Democratic National Committee I'm going to attend. It's too depressing.

There may have been American political parties in sorrier condition than the Democrats are right now—the Whigs come to mind—but there has never been a party in control of both houses of Congress that has been rendered so feeble in a single stroke.

The Democratic Party is going to have to go to prisons and offer pardons to get somebody to run against George Bush in 1992. Failing that, the Democratic candidate will have to campaign with a bag on his head.

It's going to be that bad. George Bush has presided over the most glittering military victory accorded the English-speaking peoples since Agincourt, 575 years ago. He can give capital gains to the rich, points of light to the poor and oil baths to herons all he wants and no one can say him nay.

He will not only keep Dan Quayle on the ticket in 1992, he will appoint Millie the dog to the Supreme Court.

There's only one way the Democrats can win the White House against a Bush-Quayle ticket in 1992: nominate Bush and Colin Powell.

I know, Bush might very well refuse the Democratic nomination; so what? There's nothing in the Constitution that says a presidential candidate has to be voluntary. The point is, a lot of Democrats (as well as Republicans with brains) who would otherwise vote for Bush the Republican would instead vote for Bush the Democrat if they could avoid the spectre of Dan Quayle in 1996.

Powell is the perfect vice-presidential choice in any case. He appeals to conservatives as a military hero, to liberals as a black, to smart people as a smart person. He has a nice smile.

(If Bush, contrary to expectation, dumps Quayle and picks Powell as a running mate, all bets are off. He will get 100 percent of the vote. Not even the hapless Dukakis will vote against him.)

Do not misunderstand me; I am happy we won the war. Even happier am I that it was a virtually bloodless victory. (I do not count the 100,000 or so dead Iraqis, of course; they are collateral damage.) As a believer in the two-party system, however, I cannot help but grieve at the political desolation left behind.

I cringe at the thought that Alan (The Human Scud) Simpson, Phil Gramm, Newt Gingrich and their ilk are going to be unleashed to follow their basest instincts. By this time next year you will think they were the ones who won the war, even though the closest any of them comes to a war hero is Gramm, who once taught political science at Texas A&M, where the students wear uniforms.

But let's look on the bright side: The Gulf war was the greatest outbreak of competence in the United States government since the Apollo man-on-the-moon program. I don't happen to agree with George Bush's Gulf policy, but give him this: he executed it brilliantly. It was a complex intertwining of politics, diplomacy and military strategy, and he was up to every challenge.

Just getting 500,000 troops over there and fighting a war without a hitch was a mammoth accomplishment. (Remember, as recently as twelve years ago we couldn't rendezvous a half dozen helicopters in the desert.) He managed to form a global coalition and keep it together, outmaneuvering even the conniving Gorby. He kept the Israelis out of the war and Egypt in. He neutralized the antiwar movement without supressing it and suppressed press coverage of the war without looking like Stalin.

It was an astonishing performance; Michael Jordan on a good night, Nureyev in his prime. I am convinced that it was his goal from the very beginning to get rid of Saddam as a force in the Middle East, and he pursued it unswervingly. When Iraq finally agreed to comply with all twelve United Nations resolutions, I half expected Mr. Bush to demand that Saddam appear at the surrender personally, wearing a dress and a babushka.

But he didn't. I guess he really is a kinder, gentler man.

Excuse me, I have to go now. A bunch of us liberals are gathering in front of the White House to practice our Tsorge Boosh cheer. As soon as I find my babushka. (1991)

War Record

We are a peace-loving people; everybody says so. Well, maybe not *everybody,* but we sure say so. Hardly a week goes by without one of our national leaders referring to Americans as a peace-loving people.

What can they be thinking of?

In the past fifty years we have fought four major wars; that is, wars that fully engaged the national attention. In addition, we have invaded Panama, Grenada and the Dominican Republic; sent troops to Lebanon (twice); given naval escort in wartime to ships in the Persian Gulf; bombed Libya; provided clandestine military support to various regimes and rebel groups in Central America; conspired in the assassination of at least three foreign heads of state; launched war planes to help thwart a coup in the Philippines and nurtured a military assault on Cuba. Those are merely the adventures that come readily to my aging mind; I'm sure there are others.

None of these wars, invasions, incursions, police actions and punitive expeditions, I hasten to point out, involved the defense of our soil (although, to be fair, World War II might qualify in that regard since it began for us with the bombing of Hawaii).

No other country in the past half-century can match our record for embracing armed conflict as a foreign policy tool.

Nor have we, for the most part, gone into these battles reluctantly. American presidents are never more popular than when they take us to war. It is only when we are perceived as losing the war that public opinion turns on them.

Ronald Reagan is credited with restoring our good opinion of ourselves largely through the mechanism of waging war on small, weak nations that couldn't fight back.

George Bush has been president two years and he's gotten us into two wars. Despite a recession, he's running an 80 percent approval rating in the polls. Already Republicans are aiming their campaign guns at Democrats who counseled delay of the present hostilities.

The fact is, we are a warlike people. I remember being shocked when General George Patton said as much. "Americans love war," he said in a famous address to his troops on the eve of battle.

He was right.

I'm not sure the soldiers involved are enthralled with war, but the people at home are invariably enthusiastic about it. They decorate the streets with ribbons and flags, as if in celebration. They say it's to show support for the troops, but it's the war that gets supported.

In theory, we conduct our wars in a civilized manner, adhering scrupulously to the rules laid down by the Geneva Convention; no targeting of civilians, no poison gas, no abuse of prisoners. In practice, we are less fastidious.

It is somewhat ironic that our bombing of that civilian bunker in Baghdad last week should have taken place virtually forty-five years to the day after the World War II fire-bombing of Dresden. It was a grim reminder of one of the darkest moments of our past.

The British, that other peace-loving people, conducted the first raids on Dresden, reducing one of the most beautiful cities of Europe to kindling. Then they came in with incendiary bombs to light the kindling. Then our bombers showed up to make sure the survivors couldn't fight the fires.

The result was a huge firestorm that killed more than 35,000 people; virtually all civilians. Dresden had no military significance to speak of. Most of the dead suffocated to death in their shelters.

There is a difference between herding civilians into rooms for the purpose of gassing them and bombing them into shelters for the purpose of suffocating them, but I'm not sure it's a moral one.

Even as we bomb Iraqi troops to pulp we are outraged at the thought that Saddam might use chemical weapons against us. He is "without a shred of human decency," we are told.

Have you heard about our air-fuel bombs? They explode above the ground, sending out a fine mist of petroleum jelly which then ignites, creating a firestorm that sucks up the oxygen over an area the size of four or five football fields, suffocating its victims, Dresden-style.

Why is that not a chemical weapon? What makes it more ethical than poison gas? You say that the difference is that air-fuel bombs are not banned by the Geneva Convention.

Oh, I see.

We are many things, some of them good, but peace-loving we are not. We are, instead, warlike creatures of self-delusion, able to convince ourselves of the nobility of our cause, no matter what means we use to pursue it. (1991)

Coming soon in your local bookstores: The Quayle Years: Mistakes Happen. *By a similar author.*